KU-126-830

Acknowledgements

The authors of the report would like to thank the Royal Irish Academy Third Sector Research Programme for providing the funding that enabled this research to be undertaken.

Within the Institute of Public Administration, we would like to thank our colleague Orla O'Donnell for conducting many of the interviews with voluntary and community organisations and 'umbrella' organisations representing groupings of voluntary and community organisations. We would also like to thank our colleagues from the Publications Division who were involved in getting the report into a publishable format.

We would particularly like to thank those individuals and organisations mentioned in Appendix 1, who gave of their time and knowledge to provide much valuable information.

Responsibility for the research findings in this report, as well as the interpretation of those findings, rests with the authors.

Richard Boyle
Michelle Butler

Autonomy v. Accountability

Managing government funding of voluntary and community organisations

Richard Boyle
Michelle Butler

This study was funded by a Royal Irish Academy
Third Sector Research Programme grant

INSTITUTE OF PUBLIC
ADMINISTRATION

First published in 2003
by the Institute of Public Administration
57–61 Lansdowne Road
Dublin 4
Ireland

www.ipa.ie

© Institute of Public Administration 2003

All rights reserved. No part of this publication may be reproduced or transmitted in any form or by any means, electronic or mechanical, including photocopying, recording or any information storage and retrieval system, without permission in writing from the publisher.

ISBN 1 902448 92 8

British Library cataloguing-in-publication data
A catalogue record for this book is available from the British Library

Cover design by M and J Graphics, Dublin
Typeset in 11 pt Adobe Garamond by Carole Lynch, Dublin
Printed by Future Print, Dublin, Ireland

Contents

CAVAN COUNTY LIBRARY
ACC No. C/200236
CLASS NO. 352.0415
INVOICE NO. 7105 IPA
PRICE €12.50

Foreword

So much of social science research, not only in and on Ireland but also throughout the western world, focuses on either the public or the private sector, or on the interfaces and appropriate boundaries between the two. Good as much of this work is, it runs a serious risk of ignoring something really important: a third sector that is neither public nor private, but which is driven by voluntary and community action. Perhaps this is because the individual motivations underlying activity in the third sector are not always easy to pigeonhole within mainstream social science analysis. But, and the present study paints a very clear picture of the situation, there can be no full understanding of any society which does not have as one of its fundamental components a comprehensive analysis of the role and activities of the third sector. This is increasingly recognised in many different fora, and for a number of reasons.

There are widely held fears that modern societies have suffered a degradation of something that people find it hard to put their finger on very precisely, but which they think of in general terms as 'community spirit', 'a sense of community', 'collective identity' and many other things besides. Almost certainly, this is why the academic notion of 'social capital' and the associated writings of people like Robert Putnam, in his widely read and even more widely cited *Bowling Alone*, have struck such a strong chord. From die-hard intellectuals to seasoned politicians unaccustomed to reading academic books, there is an increasing recognition that a society that does not both foster and harness the feelings that generate social and community action is a degraded society.

So the present study could not have come at a better time. The Royal Irish Academy, taking up a challenge offered by a generous private donor, has been administering a well-funded research programme focused exclusively on the third sector. As chair of the committee overseeing this activity, I have been both gratified and very pleasantly surprised by the extraordinarily high quality of the applications for research funding in this field. Many very good applications simply could not be funded; those that were funded were the cream of an excellent crop. Richard Boyle and Michelle Butler's illuminating study was one of these.

This study deals with the interaction between the public sector and the community and voluntary sector. As we can immediately see from the scale of third sector funding involved, this is an enormously important matter by any standards. In turn, this poses an enormously important problem that is the main concern of this study. How can we reap the undoubted benefits of third sector activities – which to a large extent derive from the independence and autonomy of that sector and the fact that it is far from being just another arm of government – while at the same time ensuring that it remains publicly accountable for its deployment of what are very substantial public funds?

There are no easy answers to this question – there never are to important problems in public policy. Nonetheless, this study teases out the issues in a most useful way and then draws the threads back together with a series of practical recommendations. In many ways, this is the best sort of public policy research – taking an important and under-investigated problem, analysing it rigorously and emerging at the end with some practical conclusions. For all of these reasons, Boyle and Butler's study genuinely fulfils the expectations of the RIA's Third Sector Research Programme when that was originally put in place. We should all congratulate the authors wholeheartedly for achieving this, not at all easy, feat.

Michael Laver
Chair, Royal Irish Academy Third Sector Research Programme

Executive summary

Background

This study focuses on the funding relationship between the voluntary and community sector and government. In 1999 the voluntary and community sector received €1.267 billion from Irish government and EU sources. This funding is channelled through a wide range of government departments and agencies. The 2000 *White Paper on a Framework for Supporting Voluntary Activity and for Developing the Relationship between the State and the Community and Voluntary Sector* identifies funding as a key item to be addressed. This study explores the funding relationship and addresses the central question of how to establish an appropriate balance between the autonomy of voluntary and community bodies and the public account-ability requirements arising from government funding of voluntary and community activities.

Chapter outline

After an introductory chapter setting out the study background and methodology, chapter 2 provides an overview of the role and organisation of the voluntary and community sector in Ireland. The very significant role played by the voluntary and community sector in Irish life is highlighted; so too is the largely ad hoc nature of relationships between the sector and government. No clear policy framework has existed to inform funding, service provision or other aspects of the relationship and although the 2000 White Paper begins to address this gap, it recognises that further work is needed.

Chapter 3 examines the changing environment governing the funding relationship between the voluntary and community sector and government. The rise of performance contracting as a tool of governance by government institutions internationally is noted; so too is the growing public concern and demands for scrutiny of the use made of resources provided from taxes. However, the dangers of accountability procedures becoming overly control-focused and mechanistic are also pointed out.

Chapters 4 and 5 examine the issue of partnership between voluntary and community organisations and government agencies and its implications for the funding relationship. In chapter 4, partnership definitions and purposes are explored. A framework model for understanding how partnerships can and should work, developed by the Institute of Public Health in Ireland, is used to highlight the main issues of concern while negotiating funding in a partnership setting. Chapter 5 examines the contribution partnership arrangements can make to addressing the issue of maintaining voluntary and community sector autonomy in the funding relationship with government. International experience with the development of compacts/accords between government and the voluntary and community sector is shown to provide one way of giving formal expression to the independent and advocacy role of voluntary and community organisations. These agreements, which may operate at national and at local levels, can further act as general guides on how the funding relationship should work in practice.

Chapters 6 and 7 explore the role of contracting in the funding relationship. In chapter 6, different types of contract are identified, ranging from competitive tender to more co-operative service-agreement-type models. The limitations and challenges of contracting, such as developing appropriate performance indicators and quality assurance procedures, are discussed. Broad support is identified in Ireland from the voluntary and community sector and government agencies for the use of service-agreement-type arrangements to bring more structure and formality to the funding relationship. Chapter 7 examines the specific issue of outcome-focused contracting in some detail, using international examples of practice to illustrate its development. While it has its own limitations, this outcome-focused approach can help give assurance to government about how public funds are being used. It can also give voluntary and community organisations greater freedom than the more traditional fee-per-item-of-service-type contract. The use of intermediate outcomes, or milestones, is identified as a practical way forward in developing outcome-focused agreements.

Finally, chapter 8 outlines the main conclusions from the study and makes recommendations for a new funding relationship.

Recommendations

A coherent framework is needed to promote and facilitate a more effective funding relationship between voluntary and community organisations and government. Three levels are envisaged for this framework. Level 1 focuses on the relationship between the voluntary and community sector and government at national level, level 2 on the relationship at sectoral/local level and level 3 on the relationship with government agencies.

National-level relationship (level 1)

It is recommended that:

- *a form of national agreement/compact/accord that sets out the broad parameters governing the relationship between the voluntary and community sector and government, including funding, be devised.* The 2000 White Paper on supporting voluntary activity contains much information that could easily translate across into an agreement if the relevant material were to be jointly developed further

- *there should be follow-up monitoring and annual reporting on the impact of the negotiated agreement to assess its usefulness in practice.*

Sectoral/local-level relationship (level 2)

It is recommended that:

- *at the sectoral (for example particular health sectors) or local (for example county and city development boards) level more detailed framework agreements be reached with the voluntary and community sector.* The Homeless Agency (2001) report on funding arrangements and the Department of Health (1996) *Enhancing the Partnership* report in relation to persons with a mental handicap provide examples of the type of agreement that can be negotiated at this level

- *the recommendations outlined by Donoghue (2002) regarding the development of a policy framework for the relationship of area health boards with voluntary organisations be adopted and also made applicable more widely to other sectoral/local-level agreements.* Donoghue's recommendations state that:
  — the policy must be designed in consultation with the voluntary sector
  — the policy must contain procedures and protocols

— the policy must contribute to and thereby address relationship building
— the policy must also include procedures and protocols to address the maintenance of standards and accountability
— a central location in each area health board must be identified for the relationship between the area health boards and voluntary organisations.

Agency-level relationship (level 3)

It is recommended that:

- *the practice of developing service agreements be adopted as the standard approach and developed to provide a particular focus on the outcomes to be achieved by voluntary and community organisations with public funds.* Figure A1 sets out the main parameters for this organisation-level relationship

- *the precise nature of the service agreement be contingent on the level of funding involved.* When the level of funding is small, the service agreement may be very short and general in nature. Where the funding amounts involved are larger, a more detailed service agreement is required

- *the service agreement should specify the agreed outputs, anticipated intermediate and final outcomes, and social capital indicators. Particular attention should be given to the development of intermediate outcomes resulting from the funding provided*

- *monitoring and evaluation procedures should cover financial indicators but also include output, outcome and social capital indicators.* The level and scope of monitoring and evaluation should be linked to the level of funding and the capacity of the voluntary and community organisation.

Concluding remarks

This study was established to contribute to thinking on the development of the funding relationship between voluntary and community organisations and government. In particular, the study identifies the challenge involved in developing a balance between ensuring the continuing autonomy of voluntary and community organisations and the public accountability requirements associated with the use of public money. Recommendations are made as to ways of addressing this challenge.

Figure A1 Parameters for an outcome-focused funding relationship

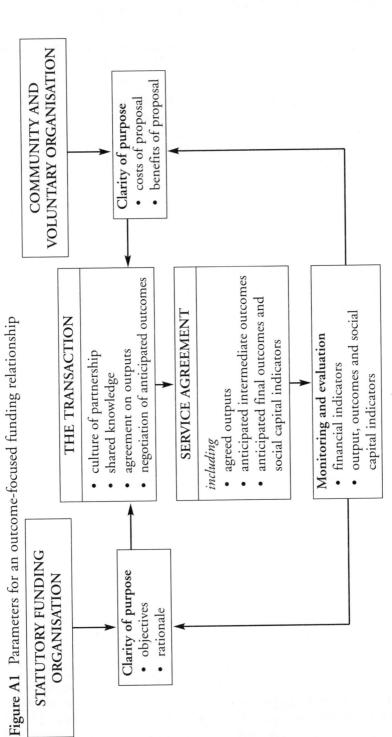

Source: adapted from Morrissey, McGinn and McDonnell (2001)

Voluntary and community organisations play a pivotal role in securing the long-term welfare of Irish society. The voluntary and community sector has made, and continues to make, a significant contribution to the main social and economic issues facing Ireland. Many public services are delivered by voluntary and community organisations on behalf of government. Enhancing the relationship between the voluntary and community sector and government is important in this context. Securing a more effective funding relationship offers benefits for both parties. In moving forward, it is important that greater clarity and structure are brought to the funding relationship, and that this is achieved through the mutual exchange of information and respect for the different perspectives involved.

1

Study background and approach

1.1 Study background

The relationship between the voluntary and community sector and government is continually evolving and developing. A critical element in this relationship is the growing government funding for the activities of the voluntary and community sector and the consequent costs, benefits and implications thereof. The voluntary and community sector often needs government funding to develop and deliver services. But at the same time, the voluntary and community sector needs freedom to respond to emerging needs and develop new services without being subject to detailed regulations and restrictions. The 2000 *White Paper on a Framework for Supporting Voluntary Activity and for Developing the Relationship between the State and the Community and Voluntary Sector* (hereafter referred to as the 2000 White Paper on supporting voluntary activity) identifies funding issues as a key item to be addressed in the relationship. A move to multi-annual funding is proposed, together with greater transparency about eligibility and application of funding. But the White Paper is relatively silent on precisely how this new funding relationship will develop, and what form it might take in practice.

Establishing an appropriate balance between the autonomy of voluntary and community bodies and the public accountability requirements of government funding poses particular challenges. The broad question to be addressed in this study is: how can the voluntary and community sector and government work together to deliver high quality, effective services, while maintaining voluntary and community sector autonomy and freedom to innovate and at the same time responding to public sector accountability requirements?

Different approaches are being tried to manage this autonomy/accountability dilemma, both nationally and internationally. Two broad approaches may be typified as management by contract and management by partnership. Management by contract is associated with new public management models of public service delivery and the move to a 'contract

1

culture' (see, for example, Boyle and Humphreys, 2001; Boston et al., 1996). Management by partnership is based on the promotion of collaborative approaches to identify and tackle shared goals (see, for example, Wilson and Charlton, 1997). Both have notable advantages and disadvantages.

Management by contract can help clarify expectations and bring a rigour to the scrutiny of publicly funded activities by voluntary and community bodies. Opponents of this approach, however, suggest that it introduces an inappropriate private sector model and mentality into the relationship between government and the voluntary and community sector (O'Ferrall, 2000). According to this thesis, too much weight is given to the accountability side of the equation and not enough to the autonomy side. Management by partnership can help to establish trust and active collaboration in the identification and achievement of service benefits. But opponents of this approach label it as too vague, allowing too much discretion. According to this thesis, too much weight is given to autonomy at the expense of accountability.

Ways of squaring the circle between management by contract and management by partnership are being developed. Instead of being seen as an 'either/or' situation, means of combining the strengths of both approaches to develop the relationship between the voluntary and community sector and government are being sought. More sophisticated models of contracting, drawing on relational contracting literature, are being developed that give equal weight to issues such as trust and collaboration and concrete expectations and deliverables (see, for example, Boyle 1993; Butler and Boyle, 2000). Similarly, an explicit focus on outcomes rather than processes is being seen as a way of achieving both accountability and autonomy (Frumkin, 2001). The aim is to free voluntary and community organisations from unnecessary restrictions, while at the same time providing assurance as to the proper use of public money.

Arising from this brief overview, two main aims for the project emerge. First, to examine existing practice in Ireland in terms of government funding of voluntary and community sector activity in the light of developments in management by contract and management by partnership as outlined above. The central thrust here is to place existing practice and thinking in the context of wider developments and to provide a framework for understanding the nature of the accountability/autonomy debate. Second, to suggest positive and practical ways forward in the funding relationship between voluntary and community organisations and the government. In particular, the research aims to highlight practical ways of managing the funding relationship which will encourage and facilitate voluntary and community sector freedom to innovate. The research thus seeks to address an issue of very practical and immediate concern to both the voluntary and community sector and the government.

1.2   Study approach and methods

This study was undertaken between October 2001 and October 2002. Over the course of the study, the research:

- reviewed existing and developing practice with regard to funding arrangements between voluntary and community organisations and the government, including determining the views of a selected number of participants from both sectors as to the strengths and weaknesses of funding arrangements and possible alternatives

- undertook a review of the national and international literature/case study material on funding relationships between governments and voluntary and community sectors, focusing particularly on contracting and partnership issues

- developed a good practice framework for funding arrangements, giving particular emphasis to balancing public accountability and the autonomy of voluntary and community organisations.

In order to carry out this work successfully, information was drawn from a number of sources:

- an extensive review of Irish and international literature, from both academic and government sources (print and Internet), in order to explore key issues, good practice and strengths and weaknesses with regard to approaches to government funding of the voluntary and community sector

- semi-structured interviews with key informants from both the voluntary and community sector and government (see Appendix 1) to help determine views as to current practice and potential future developments with regard to government funding

- interviews with a small number of cases of voluntary and community organisations and umbrella organisations representing groupings of voluntary and community organisations that are developing their funding relationships with government. These cases were selected on the basis of providing particular insights into the autonomy/accountability dilemma (see Appendix 1).

While the interviews with key informants and with selected voluntary and community organisations provide significant insights and information, it is important to note that this is in no way a representative sample of the views of the voluntary and community sector. Such a representative sampling approach was not possible or deemed relevant given the nature and scope of this research. However the interviews conducted do provide in-depth information on the central issues under investigation.

1.3   Report structure

Chapters 2 and 3 set out the broad context for the study. Chapter 2 provides an overview of the role and organisation of the voluntary and community sector in Ireland. Chapter 3 explores the changing environment governing the funding relationship between the voluntary and community sector and government.

Chapters 4 and 5 examine the issue of partnership between the voluntary and community sector and government and its implication for funding. Chapter 4 sets out definitions of partnership and examines the development of partnership relationships between government and the voluntary and community sector. Chapter 5 looks at the role of formal compacts/accords between government and the voluntary and community sector in setting an agreed context for funding.

Chapters 6 and 7 investigate the issue of contracting. Chapter 6 examines the impact of contractual relationships on funding between the voluntary and community sector and government. Chapter 7 looks at moves towards outcome-focused contracts.

Finally, in chapter 8 a framework is established to govern the funding relationship between the voluntary and community sector and government. This framework draws together the partnership and contractual elements identified in the study as key to the development of a successful funding relationship.

2

The role and organisation of the voluntary and community sector in Ireland

2.1   Introduction

In order to set the scene for this study, this chapter explores the developing role of voluntary and community organisations in Irish society. The chapter begins by examining definitions of the voluntary and community sector and exploring the substantial contribution made by voluntary and community organisations and the increasing recognition of this contribution. In the latter part of the chapter, issues relating to the relationship between statutory and voluntary and community organisations are discussed, with a particular focus on the 2000 White Paper on supporting voluntary activity.

2.2   Describing the voluntary and community sector

What is the voluntary and community sector? The clearest answer to this question arises from the seminal work of Donoghue, Anheier and Salamon (1999) in defining the nonprofit sector and the voluntary and community sector as a subset within the nonprofit sector. Organisations belonging to the nonprofit sector are identified on the basis of being:

- *organised:* they have an institutional presence and structure
- *private or non-governmental:* they are institutionally separate from government
- *non-profit-distributing:* they do not return profits to their managers or to a set of owners
- *self-governing:* they are fundamentally in control of their own affairs
- *voluntary:* membership is not legally required and such organisations attract some level of voluntary contribution of time or money.

In subsequently defining the voluntary and community sector, using categories derived from an international comparative project, Donoghue, Anheier and Salamon (1999) note:

> The voluntary and community sector . . . excludes hospitals, hospices, primary, secondary and tertiary educational institutions. It includes voluntary and community organisations in the following ICNPO (International Classification of Non Profit Organisations) categories and subcategories: culture and arts, sports and recreation, education, research, nursing homes, mental and other health, social services, emergency and relief, income support and maintenance, community development, housing, employment and training, civic and advocacy, legal, foundations, international activities and religion.

Faughan (1990) highlights the diversity found in the voluntary sector in Ireland and describes the sector as one:

> . . . that defies precise description and lacks clear boundaries . . . [and] encompasses the myriad of small, often loosely organised groups as well as the large highly professional and bureaucratic agencies. At one end of the spectrum it merges with the informal systems of help provided by relatives, friends and neighbours. At the other, it shares many of the characteristics of the public and indeed commercial sectors.

Despite this diversity, O'Sullivan (1994) suggests that a set of general characteristics of voluntary organisations can be identified:

- they have an indispensable role in any society, responding to a great variety of human needs

- in a democratic society, they facilitate participation in social and political life

- because they lack statutory responsibilities, they have a greater opportunity to adopt a pioneering and innovative role and to have flexibility in responding to need

- they have access to a large volunteer resource that is not available in the same way to the statutory sector

- they enjoy greater freedom to comment on current issues than the statutory sector and therefore contribute to public debate

- they are able to reach individuals in society – to go beyond the statistics or policy jargon to the lived reality of individual persons or communities.

Faughan (1990) identifies six categories of voluntary and community organisations in Ireland.

1. *Mutual support and self-help organisations:* based on exchange and involvement around a common interest or need. The services that they provide are based around support, information and counselling. These organisations may be focused on a single issue which is relatively constant or may have a wide or changing agenda. Many are national organisations organised as a network of local groups around the country. Faughan also reports that some started out as self-help organisations but moved increasingly into the provision of services (such as the Irish Wheelchair Association), whereas others were established as an alternative to the services model dominating the field at the time.

2. *Local development associations:* organisations 'firmly focused on a particular geographical community and on promoting its development through collective action'. The process followed is central to this category and will involve local people in defining their own needs, determining how these can best be met and combining their skills, talents and commitment to respond. Their concern for citizens' rights, self-determination and development distinguishes them from locally based service organisations. Examples of local development organisations given by Faughan include: community councils, community co-operatives and tenants' associations. She also notes that this type of voluntary organisation often cuts across the boundaries of statutory organisations in an effort to develop an integrated response to local needs.

3. *Resource and service-providing organisations:* play a major role in either complementing and supplementing government provision or as the dominant or sole provider of particular services. This is the largest category of voluntary activity in Ireland with the largest number of volunteers and people employed and it generates substantial finance from a variety of sources. It is also the area with the greatest diversity:

   - organisations differ in the geographical areas they serve – some have a distinct local focus, whereas others serve wider areas or operate at both national and local levels. Many of the larger national organisations employ staff in central or regional offices supported by a network of local branches composed exclusively of volunteers. Some national organisations comprise large numbers of local, relatively autonomous committees, with their own identity, delivering their own services and raising their own funds

- organisations differ in the nature of the service offered – some provide a comprehensive package of services for the needs of specific groups, whereas others focus on a specific service or the provision of a service or resource to other groups, for example autonomous groups working in disadvantaged areas

- in some areas, voluntary organisations are the dominant provider of basic services, for example residential services for children and almost all services for mentally handicapped persons.

4. *Representative and co-ordinating organisations:* organisations acting as umbrella groups. These are often national bodies acting as a central co-ordinating and resource agent to a membership of affiliated organisations and as a liaison point for government and public relations. They often operate at one step removed from the grass roots activity in which the affiliated organisations are involved. The organisations represented may all be voluntary or may be a mixture of voluntary and statutory organisations. Representative and co-ordinating organisations may flourish at national, regional and local level, and may in turn be affiliated at international level. All such organisations offer a forum for individuals and organisations in a particular field to come together, although the co-ordinating function is exercised with varying degrees of effectiveness. For many, there is a high priority on identifying and representing the views of affiliated organisations and trying to influence public policy development. Organisations may undertake research and produce policy documents to help inform decision making within affiliated groups and at government level. The provision of information is given high priority and many organisations also provide education and training resources.

5. *Campaigning bodies:* active campaigning may be a dimension of the work of representative organisations or may be the dominant role of an organisation. In the latter case, the primary or exclusive thrust is to bring about change through influencing legislation, policy and practice. They may be national federations where groups coalesce around a particular issue, perhaps across a wide variety of interests, or individual organisations operating as pressure groups.

6. *Funding organisations:* charitable foundations, trusts and funds, which raise funds and distribute them to particular programmes or initiatives.

Voluntary organisations also vary in terms of the ways in which volunteers are used and the degree to which organisations depend on the input of volunteers for the provision of services and the generation of funds. 'Volunteers certainly form the mainstay of many voluntary organisations in Ireland while in others their role is marginal and confined mainly to fund raising' (Faughan, 1990). Faughan also reports variations in the selection, deployment and training of volunteers.

2.3   The importance of the voluntary and community sector

Donoghue, Anheier and Salamon (1999) indicate the importance of the voluntary and community sector to the Irish economy. They note that in 1995 expenditure in the voluntary and community sector amounted to 2.14 per cent of GDP and 2.4 per cent of GNP and that 6 per cent of the non-agricultural labour force worked (in both a paid and an unpaid capacity) in the voluntary and community sector.

In 1999 the voluntary and community sector received €1.267 billion from Irish government and EU sources (see Appendix 2). This funding is channelled through a wide range of government departments, with the Department of Health and Children/health boards and the Department of Enterprise, Trade and Employment/FÁS accounting for 75 per cent between them.

Harvey and Williamson (1999) highlight the reliance of government on voluntary and community organisations to provide solutions to some of the most difficult problems facing the country. This view is supported by Faughan and Kelleher (1993), who also state that, despite this reliance, voluntary and community organisations in the early 1990s lacked 'meaningful Government recognition which would facilitate and support an appropriate response'. They go on to note that:

> There are problems concerning the level of funding and the security of funding . . . [and] no formal structure through which the voluntary and community sector can have a real voice in policy development at any level. Furthermore, statutory policy towards the voluntary and community sector is inconsistent.

2.4   The relationship between government and the voluntary and community sector

The relationship between government and the voluntary and community sector is the main area of interest of this study. Hayes (1999) suggests that government and the voluntary sector have occupied an uneasy, mutually dependent relationship, one where government depends on the voluntary sector to supplement its own service input, and where the voluntary sector depends on government to a large degree for funding and sectoral regulation. Hayes explores the notion of government as an 'uncommitted partner' – distancing voluntary organisations from decision making and 'trapping them in a continuing "client" relationship' (quoting Hogan, 1994). The limited and largely ad hoc role of voluntary organisations in policy development and planning is highlighted. Also noted is the lack of a clear policy framework that outlines precisely how voluntary organisations fit into the overall scheme of things, and how the voluntary sector can plan and deliver its services in a coherent and co-ordinated way.

The relationship between government and the voluntary and community sector can thus be explored on several levels relating to: service provision, funding, regulation and the policy framework within which the relationship evolves.

2.4.1   Service provision

The mix of statutory and voluntary provision varies between sectors. O'Sullivan (1999) suggests that in the health and education sectors, voluntary organisations function along such similar lines to statist mechanisms for welfare delivery that they could be considered to be part of a 'shadow state'. In addition, within some sectors there are areas where almost all basic services are provided by voluntary organisations, for example residential services for children and service provision for persons with mental handicap. Ironically though, in areas where voluntary organisations are the dominant providers of basic services, funding is primarily through public financing on a formalised basis (Faughan, 1990).

2.4.2   Funding

Faughan and Kelleher (1993) highlight funding as a central theme in the relationship between statutory and voluntary sectors:

> Funding is a very significant aspect of the relationship between voluntary organisations and state agencies . . . Negotiation, transfer and accounting for funds is the most visible, and for many organisations, the primary way in which the state and the voluntary sector interact.

Sources of funding for the voluntary sector include: central government departments or local or regional health, housing or educational authorities; or it may be mediated through statutory agencies with specific responsibilities in a certain area, such as tackling poverty. Funding may take the form of a discretionary grant, budget financing or per capita provision, and may derive from the exchequer, lottery funding or the EU (Faughan and Kelleher, 1993).

It is important to acknowledge that there is considerable variation between individual agencies in terms of their dependency on statutory funding. Faughan and Kelleher (1993), in a study of 46 voluntary organisations, indicate that 55 per cent of organisations received between 50 and 100 per cent of their funding from statutory sources. They note that 33 per cent of organisations received funding from health boards, 28 per cent from FÁS, 20 per cent from four government departments (Education, Health, Justice and Social Welfare) and 7 per cent from a local authority or vocational education committee. Eleven per cent of organisations did not receive statutory funding.

More generally, Donoghue, Anheiner and Salamon (1999) note that in 1995 just over half of cash income to the voluntary and community sector came from public sources. The amount varied between different parts of the sector, with public funding of over 90 per cent of cash income for education, environment and development organisations. They also note that the imputed value of volunteering is worth well over half the revenue from cash sources, indicating the importance of volunteering for the sector.

O'Sullivan (1999) reports a substantial increase in government funding for the voluntary sector which has resulted in the emergence of new contractual relationships. He suggests that the trend of increasing dependency on statutory funding is in keeping with trends in the US and the UK.

Duffy (1993) suggests that despite the extent of research on funding voluntary groups, the relationship between the statutory and voluntary sectors has not yet been clarified. Faughan and Kelleher (1993) note the lack of government policies for voluntary sector activities, which they suggest cannot be separated from the lack of formal recognition of the work of voluntary organisations. They found that this lack of a formal policy framework had particular implications for resourcing the voluntary sector and for day-to-day relationships between voluntary and government agencies. They also found that the majority of voluntary and community organisations were very dependent on government for financial resources but that their work was hampered by the frequently ad hoc and insecure nature of funding arrangements and the absence of a clear commitment from a government agency. Frequently, funding failed to match the needs of the organisation (more often related to the framework within which funding occurred rather than the level or amount of funding). The lack of coherent policies is also linked to the issue of organisations whose terms of reference for programmes span the brief of several agencies.

In terms of the impact of the absence of a clear policy framework on funding, Faughan and Kelleher (1993) report that in many cases funding arrangements depend on individual organisations negotiating on a one-to-one basis with government officials. Further, they observe that funding arrangements are often the result of 'knowing the right person, making the right contact, being in the right place at the right time, rather than being funded because there was a clear policy to promote particular activities or programmes'. They also found this to be reflected in inequitable funding arrangements for organisations providing similar services, and 'bizarre' arrangements where some projects were funded by 'totally inappropriate' government departments.

2.4.3   Regulation

Hayes (1999) reports that there is 'relatively little' statutory control over voluntary organisations. She also claims that there is no requirement on voluntary organisations to register with any statutory bodies and that the role of the Commissioners for Charitable Donations and Bequests (at that time, the body with most involvement in this area) is very limited. She claims that organisations who register as charities do so mainly out of self-interest – to qualify for tax exemptions, to reclaim tax or to qualify for statutory grants which are only payable to registered charities.

Hayes (1999) suggests that the low level of statutory regulation of Irish charities may relate to the origins of many charities, where 'typically, a group of individuals came together to tackle a particular social problem not being addressed by the state'. Generally the issue of accountability to external funders did not arise as these organisations tended to rely on their own pooled resources to finance their operations. In addition, she suggests, the religious base of many charities 'assumed a level of trust which was not seen to necessitate external scrutiny'. However she also identifies the lack of political will to take action in this area as a factor to be considered.

The Law Society's Law Reform Committee (2002) recommend major changes in the way charities are registered. The creation of a Charities Office and a Registrar of Charities is recommended, with which all charitable organisations with an annual turnover of over €2,000 would have to register. Charities would also have to file annual accounts and the Charities Office would be empowered to investigate cases of suspected fraud or misconduct.

2.4.4   Development of a policy framework

The absence of a coherent policy framework for voluntary and community sector/government relationships has been observed several times already. Donoghue (2002) notes that despite the long history of statutory–voluntary relationships in the health sector 'a lack of a policy characterises the relationship between the (former Eastern Health) Board and the voluntary sector'. She goes on to note that 'the lack of procedures on standards of accountability and on criteria for funding contributes to an absence of clarification of roles within the relationships'. The National Council for the Elderly in 1993 identified three key elements to be considered when developing a statutory–voluntary policy framework (O'Sullivan, 1994):

- *the identification of core services and the rationalisation of administrative services and levels of funding available for voluntary bodies willing to provide them:* this would involve identifying a particular set of core services that must be provided, whether by statutory organisations or voluntary organisations or both. As a result of this, voluntary organisations would receive guaranteed funding for services, and where a service is defined as a core service, they would be fully funded. O'Sullivan suggests that the statutory view is that such funding must be on the basis of negotiated contracts between statutory and voluntary organisations. Clear criteria for the provision of core services, eligibility and the provision of earmarked funding would also have to be established

- *the fostering of an ethos of statutory–voluntary partnership at both national and local levels:* the development of formal contracts between statutory and voluntary organisations could be one dimension of partnership. Further, O'Sullivan emphasises that partnership needs to recognise the specific characteristics of both the statutory and voluntary sectors, and that the views of users should inform the priorities set by organisations and the development of statutory–voluntary links

- *the creation of a context and a structure for the planned development of the voluntary sector:* O'Sullivan links this concept closely to the develop-ment of a statutory–voluntary partnership and suggests that the long-term development of this partnership can only occur if there is a clear policy commitment to the promotion of the voluntary sector, and if better co-ordinated structures are developed within the voluntary sector. However, he suggests that there is a contradiction, in theory at least, between the notion of a planned development of the voluntary sector and the concept of an autonomous voluntary sector. Further, he points out that the voluntary sector must also take responsibility for its own development, which involves the development of structures and of skills and supports to ensure such structures are used.

A key element of any voluntary and community sector/statutory policy framework is that of partnership. One of the core policy concepts seeking to re-orient the Irish health system that O'Ferrall (2000) identifies in the 1994 health strategy, *Shaping a Healthier Future*, is the development of a partnership between statutory health agencies and voluntary agencies. The strategy envisages that, through partnership, health authorities will be responsible for funding all providers within their areas. Health authorities will link funding to agreed levels of service to be provided through service agreements with voluntary providers. In order to ensure continuity, service agreements will be for terms of a number of years but funding will be agreed on an annual basis. The development of this new statutory framework for partnership is aimed at recognising the roles and responsibilities of both statutory and voluntary sectors while fully respecting the independent identity of voluntary agencies and enabling them to retain their autonomy. It is also aimed at replacing the direct funding of voluntary agencies by the Department of Health, an arrangement that was seen to impede the proper co-ordination and development of services at local level. In a similar manner, *Enhancing the Partnership* (Department of Health, 1996), developed in consultation with the voluntary mental health agencies, seeks to address the issue of the autonomy and independence of the voluntary sector and develop the practice of service agreements.

2.5   *White Paper on a Framework for Supporting Voluntary Activity and for Developing the Relationship between the State and the Community and Voluntary Sector*

The 2000 White Paper on supporting voluntary activity aims to address many of the issues raised in section 2.4. In particular it acknowledges that the legal and policy framework to support voluntary work and the contexts in which it takes place is underdeveloped. The White Paper represents a start to the government's commitment to dealing with the situation. The 'vision' set out in the White Paper is:

> The rapidly changing economic and social situation in Ireland requires serious consideration on how to influence society and make it socially and economically inclusive, to make it a place where equality of

treatment, opportunity and access, and respect for autonomy of the individual are the norm. There is a need to create a more participatory democracy where active citizenship is fostered.

Accordingly, five key principles are outlined:

- *active citizenship:* the active role of people, communities and voluntary organisations in decision making which directly affects them; thereby moving towards direct democratic participation and responsibility

- *resource allocation and promotion of equality of opportunity:* addressing the underlying structural causes of exclusion of some groups from opportunities and resources available to the rest of society

- *helping people to participate in issues which affect them:* developing positive action programmes to target groups that are most marginalised and to support them to be involved in issues and concerns affecting them and their communities

- *respect for individual freedom in the pursuit of social goals:* fostering a culture that respects the autonomy of the individual. This means creating a climate which supports individuals and groups to make things happen rather than have things happen to them

- *promoting and strengthening social dialogue:* facilitating individuals and communities to speak out about the problems affecting them and to be part of the practical response. The promotion and strengthening of social dialogue across society involves government developing partnerships with a wide range of bodies and organisations, including not only voluntary and community interests but also employer representatives, trade unions and farming organisations.

Building on these principles, a range of practical measures are proposed in the 2000 White Paper to ensure better government support for voluntary and community organisations:

- formal recognition of the role of the voluntary and community sector in contributing to the creation of a vibrant, participative democracy and civil society

- introduction of mechanisms in all relevant public service areas for consultation with voluntary and community sector groups and to allow the communities they represent have an input into policy making

- multi-annual funding to become the norm for agreed priority services and community development activities. This will mean a major move away from the present unsatisfactory and ad hoc funding schemes experienced by many voluntary and community groups

- designation of voluntary activity units in relevant government departments to support the relationship with the voluntary and community sector

- holding of regular policy fora by relevant departments and agencies to allow for wider consultation and participation by the voluntary and community sector in the policy-making process

- best practice guidelines in relation to consultation by statutory agencies with the voluntary and community sector and in relation to funding mechanisms and systems, to which all government departments and statutory agencies will be expected to adhere

- a strong government commitment to follow up and implement all the decisions in the White Paper. An Implementation and Advisory Group, drawn from relevant government departments, statutory agencies and the voluntary and community sector itself, has been established to oversee the implementation of the White Paper decisions and to pursue other issues that arise

- transfer of responsibility for charity regulatory matters and the Commissioners of Charitable Donations and Bequests to the Department of Social and Family Affairs

- an ongoing review of funding programmes and schemes, to be carried out by the Implementation and Advisory Group working under the aegis of the Cabinet Committee on Social Inclusion, to bring about a more coherent and user-friendly system of funding and support. The long-term aim is to change from the existing, highly fragmented funding and support system to one based on the concept of single line funding and single line reporting mechanisms.

However, the White Paper is not the final word on a policy framework, and indeed has its own limitations. Donoghue (2002) notes that the White Paper:

... does not cover all voluntary and community organisations in Ireland but focuses quite specifically on organisations with an anti-poverty remit. There is a possibility, too, that the White Paper may be perceived as a policy on the relationship between the [then] Department of Social, Community and Family Affairs and certain voluntary and community organisations rather than on voluntary–statutory relationships in general.

2.6   Conclusions

The very significant role played by the voluntary and community sector in Irish life is highlighted in this chapter. The findings show that, historically, relationships between the voluntary and community sector and government have been largely ad hoc in nature. No clear policy framework has existed to inform funding, service provision or other aspects of the relationship. The 2000 White Paper on supporting voluntary activity begins to address this issue and recognises that greater clarity is needed in terms of funding and accountability relationships between government and the voluntary and community sector.

3

A changing environment
for the funding relationship

3.1   Introduction

Before examining in detail the nature of the funding relationship between
voluntary and community organisations and the government, it is
necessary to understand the context within which this relationship occurs.
While chapter 2 set the general scene by exploring the role of voluntary and
community organisations in Irish society, it is important to note that, both
domestically and internationally, the management of government, the role
of the voluntary and community sector and theoretical understandings of
government/voluntary and community sector relations are changing.
These changes have important implications for the accountability of
voluntary and community organisations for their use of public funds and
more generally for the nature of the funding relationship itself.

3.2   The changing nature of government, voluntary and community organisations and theoretical understandings of government/voluntary and community sector relations

3.2.1   Changes in the management of government

Public service management practice has changed significantly over the last
twenty years. In countries such as the US and the UK change was driven
initially by a 'new right' agenda of rolling back the state, privatisation and
the importation of business management practices. Subsequently public
management reforms have tended to focus on issues such as strategic
management, devolution and decentralisation of responsibilities and the
management of cross-cutting issues (for more details, see Boyle, 1995 and
Boyle and Humphreys, 2001). Of particular concern to this study are
two important and inter-related developments: a growth in performance

contracting and an increasing emphasis on the management of networks rather than hierarchies.

Performance contracting is seen as providing 'a framework for generating desired behaviours in the context of devolved management structures' (OECD, 1999). Given new arrangements for the management and delivery of services (privatisation, contracting out, decentralisation), performance contracting is seen by many administrations as a useful way in which to achieve a clear definition of objectives and to support management control, while also leaving managers freedom with regard to day-to-day activities. The OECD (1999), in a review of performance contracting, note that 'performance contracts include a range of management instruments used within the public sector to define responsibilities and expectations between parties to achieve mutually agreed results'. Performance contracting is also seen as an important tool in ensuring accountability for the use of public money in decentralised service delivery scenarios.

Managing networks of organisations involved in public service provision is part of a move from government to governance (Boyle and Humphreys, 2001). While government agencies are still key actors in service delivery, there is increasing involvement of others and the role of the private and nonprofit sectors is growing. An increasing voice for civil society is a common espoused value in many countries. There is recognition that government cannot act alone, but must interact with markets, voluntary organisations, civil society and individual citizens to deal with issues of public concern. A decreasing emphasis on management through hierarchies and an increasing focus on managing complex networks is an important part of this process. In this setting, public service managers:

> . . . need a much greater tolerance for ambiguity, a willingness to take considerable risks, and to manage a myriad of different professional cultures in their search for co-operation between the constituent elements of the network. Moreover, they will need to be expert brokers of contracts and builders of trust (Jackson and Stainsby, 2000).

3.2.2   Changes in the role of the voluntary and community sector

The concept of active citizenship is highlighted in the 2000 White Paper on supporting voluntary activity, which defines it as:

> . . . the active role of people, communities and voluntary organisations in decision-making which directly affects them. This extends the

concept of formal citizenship and democratic society from one of basic
civil, political and social and economic rights to one of direct
democratic participation and responsibility.

With regard to this concept of active citizenship, voluntary and community
organisations are playing an increasingly prominent role in contributing to
policy thinking in national and local partnership arenas. In Ireland, the
representation of the voluntary and community sector in the development
of national partnership programmes, *Partnership 2000* (1996) and the
Programme for Prosperity and Fairness (2000), are expressions of this
development. Similar developments are also evident in other countries, for
example Canada and Australia (National Institute for Governance, 2001).

At the same time, voluntary and community organisations in Ireland,
along with others internationally, are increasingly active in speaking out on
behalf of their constituencies and clients in public policy debates. This
advocacy role has long been a feature of many voluntary and community
organisations, but it has grown in importance as governments more
actively involve the private and nonprofit sectors in service delivery. The
advocacy role has also increased as pressures grow from government off-
loading services or as increasing inequalities in society are identified.

Voluntary and community organisations are also caught up in the
general decline in trust in all public institutions that is occurring in Ireland
and elsewhere (see, for example, Panel on Accountability and Governance
in the Voluntary Sector, 1999 for Canadian experience). Although the
public in general has a high regard for the voluntary and community sector,
there is a sense that more scrutiny is needed of how the sector works and
how it spends the money it receives from donations and public funding.

3.2.3   *Changes in the theoretical underpinning of government/ voluntary and community sector relations*

Various economic and organisational theories can be helpful in understanding how governments and voluntary and community sectors interact.
Theoretical developments are aimed at enhancing our understanding of
why governments interact with voluntary and community sectors and how
to secure the most effective interaction.

Weisbrod (1977), in exploring the voluntary nonprofit sector,
introduced the notion of 'government failure' to explain why nonprofit
organisations provide collective goods on a voluntary basis. The argument
here is that governments, when determining the quantity and quality of
public goods to be provided, follow the preferences of the median voter or

a dominant political coalition. Given the need for equity, services are provided in a standardised manner. If citizen preferences are not homogeneous, some citizens will be left unsatisfied, leaving a gap to be filled by the nonprofit sector in the provision of public-good services. Nonprofit organisations in this scenario can be seen as supplements to government (Young, 2000), ensuring greater diversity and customisation of service provision. This theory of government failure helps explain why voluntary and community organisations are involved in providing niche public services that meet particular needs.

Government failure is also useful in understanding the advocacy role played by voluntary and community organisations. As Young (2000) notes:

> In heterogeneous communities, where minority views are not well reflected in public policy, minorities will organise themselves on a voluntary collective basis, not only to provide public services for themselves but also to press government to more adequately serve their interests.

There is also a theory of 'voluntary failure' that helps explain why governments may need to either provide services themselves or intervene to regulate the operation of the voluntary and community sector. Salamon (1987) outlines four voluntary failures:

- *philanthropic insufficiency:* related to the limited scale and resource base of the voluntary and community sector

- *philanthropic particularism:* concerning the tendency of voluntary and community organisations to focus on particular groups or projects to the exclusion of others

- *philanthropic paternalism:* concerning the fact that those who control the resources can choose whom to serve

- *philanthropic amateurism:* as opposed to professional service provision.

In these circumstances governments are seen as more equitable, professional, democratic and inclusive.

Salamon (1995) has been the principal advocate of the view that the voluntary and community sector plays a complementary rather than supplementary role in the provision of services. In this scenario, governments finance public services, while voluntary and community organisations deliver them. Transaction cost theory (see Boyle, 1995) helps explain why in many circumstances it may be more efficient for governments to delegate the delivery of public services to nonprofit organisations rather than deliver them directly. In brief, governments may choose to contract out services because it is cheaper than expanding work internally. Contracting with nonprofit organisations provides two particular advantages: (a) voluntary and community organisations are knowledgeable about their individual communities and therefore services can, within limits, be tailored to local needs more effectively and (b) because they are nonprofit organisations the monitoring costs of contracting out are reduced. Young (2000) summarises the position:

> In all, the theory of public goods coupled with the theory of transaction costs provides a plausible explanation for why government and nonprofits often engage in a complementary relationship in which government finances and nonprofits deliver services. This relationship is more likely to be observed in areas such as social services, where free riding is a significant problem, where direct public production is likely to require a large bureaucratic operation, and where differences in local preferences favour some differentiation of services to alternative locales and consumer groups.

These theoretical underpinnings of government and voluntary and community sector relations are important in enhancing understanding of practical issues such as why and how contracting relationships develop, why governments may sometimes choose to fund activity provided by voluntary and community organisations and why sometimes governments prefer to provide services themselves. As Brinkerhoff and Brinkerhoff (2002) note, these theoretical developments:

> . . . enhance understanding of how governments and nonprofits interact, and whether their interactions provide responsive, accountable and efficient solutions to societal problems that no single sector can address independently. This consideration involves more than just public service delivery arrangements. It raises questions of democracy, citizenship, representation, equity, and values that concern the appropriate boundary between state and society.

3.2.4　Conclusions regarding the changing environment for government funding of voluntary and community organisations

The above brief discussion has highlighted a number of important environmental changes and theoretical underpinnings that impact on the funding relationship between government and voluntary and community organisations.

From the perspective of government, management reforms and in particular the growth of performance contracting are shaping thinking about the nature of the relationship between government agencies and voluntary and community organisations. There is an increasing emphasis on the need to specify and identify what will be delivered in return for public money rather than simply handing over a grant. Also, the active participation of voluntary and community organisations as part of a partnership network of organisations involved in the delivery of services is receiving growing prominence.

From the perspective of voluntary and community organisations, there is a balance to be maintained between their increasingly direct role in policy development and implementation through the promotion of active citizenship, and maintaining an independent advocacy voice for the individuals and groups they represent. At the same time, voluntary and community organisations are under increasing public scrutiny in their use of funds.

A recent Canadian review indicates some of the implications of these changes:

> Voluntary organisations have had to respond to these challenges in order to survive and thrive. From the smallest and informal to the largest and most sophisticated organisations, leaders in the sector have been thinking about how to be more responsive, how to do more (and better) with less, and how to work in more transparent ways. A central aspect of this self-assessment involves examining the basic principles of governance and accountability (Panel on Accountability and Governance in the Voluntary Sector, 1999).

3.3   The changing nature of accountability

Given the general trends outlined above, accountability is a growing issue for voluntary and community organisations. In the context of this study, it is accountability for the use of public funds which is the focus. In the past, accountability was not seen as such a major issue. There were two main reasons for this, one rooted in morality and the other in economic theory. Morally, voluntary and community organisations were, in a sense, trusted largely because of their good intentions. The fact that they were set up to 'do good works' was seen as providing an accountability mechanism. With regard to economic theory, Hansmann (1980) outlines what he terms the 'nondistribution constraint' acting on nonprofit organisations:

> . . . an organisation is barred from distributing its net earnings, if any, to individuals who exercise control over it, such as members, officers, directors or trustees . . . Net earnings, if any, must be retained and devoted in their entirety to financing further production of services that the organisation was formed to provide.

This nondistribution constraint is seen as an important element in ensuring that nonprofit organisations act as they should. As such, the argument goes, the constraint itself acts as an accountability mechanism, reducing the need for other forms of accountability. As the profit element is absent, there is no logical reason or incentive for the nonprofit organisation to misuse the funds allocated to it.

However, changes such as the increasing focus by government on how public funds are being used and the general reduction in trust in public institutions, including voluntary and community organisations, have led to demands for more formal accountability for the sector. Boyle (1998a) notes that there are two broad aspects involved in ensuring public accountability:

- giving an account, in terms of providing information and explaining the actions of the organisation so that the use of public funds is open to scrutiny
- being held to account, in terms of responding to comments and criticisms made, and taking the views of stakeholders on board.

These two aspects of accountability raise a number of questions as to how accountability is applied in practice to the use of public funds by voluntary and community organisations. These questions are addressed below.

Accountability to whom?

While the focus of this study is on the funding relationship between government agencies and voluntary and community organisations, it is important to note that voluntary and community organisations are accountable to a wide range of stakeholders. These include clients, members, donors and staff as well as the general public. They are accountable in different ways to these interests. The funding accountability relationship has to be set within this wider context.

Accountability for what?

Pollitt (1999) identifies three main aims defining an accountability relationship between an accountor (who gives account) and an accountee (who receives it) in the public sector:

- *control:* where the focus is on the accountor showing compliance with procedures and control of abuse. The main interest here is in ensuring probity in the use of public funds

- *assurance:* where the focus is on demonstrating that the organisation is functioning as intended, in terms of the pursuit of plans and commitments. The main interest here is accounting for the processes and activities used to deliver services provided by public funds

- *performance improvement:* where the focus is on showing economy, efficiency and effectiveness in the running of the organisation. The main interest here is on accounting for the outcomes achieved through the use of public funding.

Pollitt also notes that the spirit of these three aims is different. A control mentality, for example, tends to place less emphasis on performance improvement. Balancing these aims, and managing the tensions between them, presents challenges for both the accountor and the accountee. From the perspective of voluntary and community organisations, traditionally more emphasis has been given by government agencies to the control and assurance aims, in terms of ensuring that the public money allocated was used for the purposes intended. Increasingly, however, the question is also being asked of the impact of that expenditure in terms of the outcomes achieved by the organisation.

Accountability by what means?

Apart from the organisational form and nondistributional constraint mechanism, voluntary and community organisations must use a variety of accountability methods to meet the demands placed on them. These include:

- social governance arrangements, often by the board of an organisation

- professional standards and accreditation

- codes of conduct and ethics

- contracts.

The degree of formality attached to such mechanisms and the reporting on their application will vary, depending on the size of the organisation and the scale of public funding involved. The smaller the organisation or the amount of public money, the less formal and onerous the subsequent accountability arrangements need to be.

3.3.1   Conclusions regarding accountability developments

Voluntary and community organisations are facing increasing accountability demands. The nonprofit nature of voluntary and community activity is no longer accepted as evidence of the prudent and effective use of public funds. Government agencies are increasingly looking for information on the outcomes achieved by voluntary and community organisations.

This downplaying of trust and increasing emphasis on checking up on the operation of organisations poses challenges for the voluntary and community sector. There is a danger of accountability becoming overly mechanistic in such circumstances, with an overburdening of regulations and reporting requirements. There is also the need to recognise the great diversity that exists in the voluntary and community sector, as illustrated in chapter 2, with a vast array of different-sized organisations with differing mandates and means of operation. Applying a single, standard accountability approach is unlikely to work in such circumstances. Rather, it is a case of choosing the most appropriate accountability arrangements from the range that is available, as described above. This needs to be done in the context of a framework that provides coherence to the funding and accountability relationship.

4

Partnership: what, why and how

4.1 Introduction

So far in this study we have identified partnership and contracting as two key elements in the funding relationship between the voluntary and community sector and government. Yet, as has been pointed out, there is potential and often real tension between these two elements. In order to understand how they can work together to enhance the funding relationship, it is important to have a better understanding of both partnership and contracting and how they work in practice. In this chapter, the social partnership model in Ireland and different definitions of partnership are explored; a framework for understanding how partnership works is outlined; and finally, using the Homeless Initiative in Dublin as a case study, the application of partnership and its implications for funding are examined.

4.2 Social partnership in Ireland: setting the scene

Before going into the evolving partnership relationship between the voluntary and community sector and government, it is important to put this relationship within the wider context of social partnership in Ireland. Social partnership, particularly through the development of national, multi-year economic and social development programmes, is widely seen as helping to deliver industrial stability and moderate pay settlements, thus contributing to competitiveness and economic growth (NESC, 1996). But as the National Economic and Social Council (NESC) also indicate, the collaboration of the social partners at national level has contributed more generally to the development of a social partnership ethos in the public policy arena (NESC, 1999).

At national level, partnership has become more encompassing through the inclusion of the voluntary and community sector on the NESC. At local level, a partnership approach is being used by county and city development boards in the devising of county strategies for economic, social and cultural development (*Preparing the Ground*, 1999). The voluntary and community sector is formally involved in the process. Similarly, the voluntary and community sector is formally involved in strategic policy committees (SPCs) in local government, which have been in operation since 2000. SPCs are intended to enhance democracy at local government level and broaden involvement in local government. At the level of the individual organisation or enterprise, partnership between employers, trade unions and staff is an objective of public policy (Boyle, 1998b).

This is not to say that social partnership is seen as a panacea. O'Donnell (2001), in a review of the future of social partnership in Ireland, indicates a sense of unease about partnership among some constituencies. The ability of social partnership to deliver a continuing stable pay and industrial relations climate and help address key public policy issues has been questioned in some instances. Ó Cinnéide (1999) has also been highly critical about the growing corporatism associated with social partnership at the expense of representative democracy. There is a sense that social partnership must evolve if it is to continue. However from the perspective of this study the main points arising from social partnership are: (a) the formal inclusion of the voluntary and community sector in the social partnership process and (b) the contribution that social partnership has made to the development of a wider ethos of partnership as a useful and effective approach to joint problem solving and decision making.

4.3   Partnership between the voluntary and community sector and government: what is it and why have it?

Partnership is a word that means different things to different people. Social partnership, mentioned above, is concerned primarily with the relationship between the main social partners (government, employers, trade unions, farmers, the voluntary and community sector). Partnership within organisations is concerned with the relationship between managers, trade unions and staff. Here, however, we are concerned with the concept of partnership in terms of the relationship between government and the voluntary and community sector, and in particular between government agencies and voluntary and community organisations, in other words our focus is on inter-organisational partnership.

A legal understanding of business partnerships indicates that all partners are jointly and severally liable for both the successes and failures of the venture. In a public service context, Kernaghan (1993) defines partnership as 'a relationship involving the sharing of power, work, support and/or information with others for the achievement of joint goals and/or mutual benefits'. Wilson and Charlton (1997) refer to partnership as 'organisations – representing the public, private and voluntary sectors – acting together by contributing their diverse resources in the furtherance of a common vision that has clearly defined goals and objectives'. More specifically from the point of view of this study, a draft guide for public/voluntary sector partnerships states that partnership exists 'where each party has an opportunity to contribute to the decisions of the partnership and to influence the provision which arises from it, be this at policy, strategic or implementation level' (Compact Working Group, 2001).

A number of key points emerge from these definitions. The notion of jointly agreed goals shared among the participants in the partnership is indicated. So too is the fact that participants have obligations under a partnership arrangement. Further, the notion of actively working together in a spirit of common interest and common ownership is stressed.

Partnership may also operate at one or a number of different levels between organisations. Gaster and Deakin (1998) have developed the concept of a ladder of partnership to illustrate the different types of partnership arrangement that may exist between local government and the voluntary sector (see Figure 4.1).

Partnerships may also address different objectives, such as the development of policy, the development of strategy or the implementation of strategy (Compact Working Group, 2001).

4.3.1 Why partnership?

Pursuing partnership as an end in itself is unlikely to be productive. Rather, it needs to be seen as a way of working that aims to address particular social, economic and environmental issues. Wilson and Charlton (1997) outline four reasons why the move to cross-sectoral partnership has increased in prominence in the 1990s:

- the political agenda is encouraging partnership developments
- partnerships are often seen as the most appropriate vehicle for addressing social and economic needs, offering greater involvement by all sectors of society in the allocation of public funds
- the notion of partnership fits in with the emerging concepts of communitarianism and a stakeholder society. Individuals and

organisations from all sectors are increasingly demanding a voice in defining and implementing responses to policy challenges

- most social problems have multiple causes and therefore need a multi-agency approach to solutions.

Figure 4.1 A ladder of partnership

Type of 'partnership'	What it might involve
Information exchange	Identifying local and service needs where cross-boundary working is needed and could be effective
Action planning	Mutual learning, knowledge of what each partner does and could do Joint problem-solving approaches to agree actions and processes Identifying (the need for) new partners
Co-ordination	Active co-ordination process: co-ordinator knows what is going on, draws on each partner as appropriate, helps to nurture development and involvement of new partners
Implementing projects and service plans	Mutual trust Identifying specific inputs from each partner Commitment to act on agreed elements
Collaboration	Joint problem solving and action Shared values and agendas
Full partnership	Shared values Pooled resources Blurred boundaries Continuously developing to meet changing needs Less powerful partners supported to play a full role

Source: Gaster and Deakin, 1998

More generally, and building on the last point above, Huxham (1995) suggests that partnership is appropriate when seeking to achieve objectives that no single organisation can achieve alone. Huxham uses the term 'collaborative advantage' to describe a situation where, through collaboration, something is achieved that no organisation could achieve on its own, and where individual organisations also achieve their own objectives better than they could alone.

However, Huxham (1995, 1996) also indicates that partnership is not without its problems and pitfalls, including:

- *loss of control:* the ability to take action if things seem to be going wrong or differently from expectations may be reduced in partnerships. The sharing of decision making may act as a constraint on actions

- *multiple goals:* specification of common goals for the partnership may cause problems, in that it can make existing differences more explicit, with the advantages of ambiguity being lost. Also, stakeholders are likely to want to achieve their own particular goals through partnerships, which may not relate to the stated purpose of the partnership

- *tensions between autonomy and accountability:* for those actively involved in partnership, autonomy of action – being able to respond to positions of the other actors in the partnership arrangement – can be important in progressing actions. Yet members may be accountable to their stakeholder groups (government departments to ministers, voluntary organisations to boards), which may mean checking back before committing to a decision. This tension can cause problems.

Thus, while partnership between the voluntary and community sector and government offers advantages as a way of working, it is not without its problems. From the perspective of the funding relationship, the positive aspects of partnership involve issues such as the development of a longer-term relationship rather than one-off funding allocations, joint decision making as to the appropriate level and use of resources and shared agreement as to the objectives which funding is aimed at achieving. The more negative aspects of partnership involve potential problems such as inertia rather than responsiveness to emerging needs, slowness of decision making and conflicts between individual organisational goals and those of the partnership with relation to funding. There is also the issue of inequality in the partnership, with smaller and more marginalised groups in particular danger of being sidelined.

There is also a close relationship between partnership and contracting. In England, 'Increasingly contracting is seen as the mechanism through which partnerships pay for the partnership agenda to be implemented or delivered' (Compact Working Group, 2001). Also, partnerships may themselves have money allocated to them, which they in turn allocate on the basis of tendered-for contracts.

4.4 A framework for partnership

If partnership between the voluntary and community sector and government is to play a role in influencing the funding relationship that exists, it is important to understand how partnerships work to achieve desired outcomes. To this end, the Institute of Public Health in Ireland (2000) have developed a framework model for understanding how partnerships work (see Figure 4.2).

Figure 4.2 The partnership framework

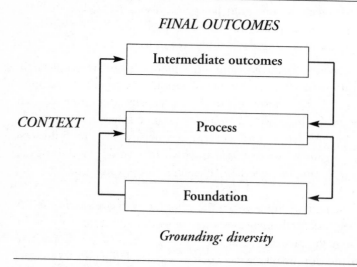

Source: adapted from Institute of Public Health in Ireland, 2000

The main elements of the model are:

1. *Context:* refers to the wider environment within which partnerships operate. It includes factors such as previous history of working together, the political climate and policies/laws/regulations.

2. *Grounding:* refers to the need for the partnership to be grounded in valuing and respecting diversity. Understanding the different perspectives of participants and managing differences of opinion constructively are key factors.

3. *Foundation:* involves building a shared purpose and strategy. The main tasks involved here are the development of:

  - vision: image of a desired future

  - mission: purpose of working together and the fundamental reason for the partnership's existence

  - principles: guidelines for style of working and decision making

  - values: the beliefs individuals and the group hold

  - measuring impact: how impact will be evaluated

  - infrastructure: how the day-to-day business will be carried out

  - contribution: making explicit what is expected from members, why they are there, how they will be held accountable and the incentives they need to stay involved.

4. *Process:* relates to the skills and dynamics of the partnership associated with building effective working relationships. Process factors include leadership, communication, team building, sustainability and research and evaluation.

5. *Intermediate and final outcomes:* outcomes refer to the difference made by partnerships; the tangible improvements to the different constituencies served by and who make up the partnership. However final outcomes (such as increased employment rates, lower alcohol and drug rates) are virtually impossible to attribute directly to the efforts of partnership alone. Consequently the framework proposes the use of intermediate outcome measures (these measures are referred to as impact measures in the Institute of Public Health model, but the term intermediate outcomes is used in this study for consistency with later references to the concept). Intermediate outcomes are measures that can be directly related to the activities and outputs of the partnership and which create the conditions necessary to achieve final outcomes. Intermediate outcomes may result in changes in people's behaviour and attitudes, policy development, systems development (improvements in co-ordination or infrastructure) and resource development (changes in social and economic capital). Outcomes may also be either expected or unexpected.

From the perspective of the funding relationship, this framework can be used to improve understanding of how negotiations on funding may occur in a partnership setting. Key issues to look out for in determining the success of the funding negotiation can be determined. For example, if the foundation is insufficient, in that not enough time has been given to agreeing the goal of the partnership, problems may occur. Similarly, joint agreement on the desired impacts and outcomes may facilitate agreement on funding needs and appropriate levels of funding.

4.5   Partnership in practice: new funding arrangements for the provision of services to the homeless in Dublin

In order to see how the partnership model outlined in Figure 4.2 can contribute to the funding relationship between the voluntary and community sector and government, it is interesting to look at the illustrative example of homelessness in Dublin. In 1996 the Homeless Initiative was established as a partnership between greater Dublin local authorities, the health board and voluntary agencies to improve the planning, co-ordination and delivery of services to the homeless (in 2002 the Initiative became the Homeless Agency: see Boyle, Butler and O'Donnell, 2001 for details of the operation of the Homeless Initiative). Using the different elements of the model, it is possible to see how a partnership approach has led to a new funding regime, one of the main priorities of the Homeless Initiative:

1. *Context:* at the time the Homeless Initiative was established, there was a perceived lack of clarity with regard to the respective statutory responsibilities of housing authorities and health boards regarding the provision of services for the homeless. Voluntary organisations were looking to develop services for the homeless, but each agency tended to operate and liaise with the statutory bodies independently. Funding for services to homeless people was fragmented and uncoordinated, with different agencies using different application forms, different procedures and different requirements in relation to monitoring and evaluation.

2. *Grounding:* over the course of the Homeless Initiative, the need for participants to understand the point of view of other participants, voluntary and statutory, was a constant challenge. A situation evolved through the establishment of improved working relationships where, while there were still disagreements, they did not prevent the work agenda moving forward. In general, close working led to a better understanding of the position of the other sector.

3. *Foundation:* much effort was put into building a shared purpose and strategy. Annual work plans for the Homeless Initiative were jointly

agreed. In relation to funding, key principles were established to underpin the new funding arrangements:

- *related to overall policy objectives:* funding will support government strategy in relation to homelessness and the achievement of the objectives of *Shaping the Future – An Action Plan on Homelessness in Dublin 2001–2003*

- *unity and coherence:* the relevant statutory funding bodies are committed to ensuring that funding in relation to homelessness is provided in a co-ordinated way, through a process to be managed by the Homeless Agency

- *transparency:* the availability of funding, the application process, how decisions are made and on what basis, will all be clearly communicated. Organisations which are turned down for funding will be given the reasons why and may request a review

- *rationality:* decisions on funding will be based on the need for specific services and the ability of organisations to deliver those services

- *adequacy:* funding will as far as possible, within the constraints of government funding, relate to the actual cost of providing services to the appropriate standard in a cost-effective way

- *related to needs:* funding will be related to meeting known and emerging needs of people who are homeless

- *accountability:* monitoring and evaluation arrangements will ensure improved accountability for expenditure of funds on homeless services, both in terms of value for money and effectiveness in addressing the needs of people who are homeless and the prevention of homelessness (Homeless Agency, 2001).

4. *Process:* a central element of progressing the work of the Homeless Initiative was the establishment of working groups. A specific working group on funding was established, including representatives from voluntary organisations, central and local government and the health agencies. This working group produced the report on new funding arrangements that was adopted by the Homeless Agency. A further key element of the process was the research work undertaken. Models of good practice in funding, both national and international, were examined. The same approach was used by a different working group to establish standards of good practice for homeless services, to which funding could be linked.

5. *Intermediate and final outcomes:* in terms of intermediate outcomes, the initial result of the exercise has been the development of jointly agreed new funding arrangements for homeless services in Dublin. The report outlining the new arrangements (Homeless Agency, 2001) sets out:

- purpose and principles of funding

- eligible services and activities

- what is included in funding (actual, overhead and capital costs)

- application process and timetable

- how applications are assessed

- monitoring and evaluation procedures

- the content items to be included in service agreements in relation to each approved application.

In 2002, €20 million of government funding was allocated under the new funding arrangements. For the first time, the full range of services to the homeless, including settlement, street outreach and day services received statutory support. Funding is subject to service agreements and monitoring, carried out by the Homeless Agency on behalf of statutory bodies. Monitoring applies to all funded services, voluntary and statutory.

It is too early as yet to assess the final outcomes of the funding arrangements, in terms of the actual impact on service provision and services to the homeless in general.

4.6   Conclusions

This brief review of partnership has identified a number of issues of significance for the funding relationship between the voluntary and community sector and government:

- the voluntary and community sector are now formally included in the social partnership process, both nationally through bodies such as the NESC and locally through, for example, strategic policy committees and county and city development boards

- partnership involves the development of jointly agreed goals, with common interest and ownership, with all parties also having obligations under the partnership arrangement. Partnership is particularly appropriate when seeking to achieve objectives that no single organisation can achieve alone

- partnership is not a panacea, and may have its own problems. These can include slowness of decision making, conflicts between individual organisational goals and partnership goals and inequity or unequal strength of participants in the partnership

- a framework for understanding how partnerships can and should work is useful. The framework model developed by the Institute of Public Health in Ireland points out key issues to be aware of when negotiating funding in a partnership setting

- partnership working can help produce jointly agreed funding arrangements between voluntary and community organisations and statutory organisations, as illustrated by the funding arrangements for homeless services in Dublin.

5

Voluntary and community sector–government compacts: formal expressions of partnership

5.1   Introduction

The partnership approach used to develop a new funding arrangement for homeless services in Dublin discussed in chapter 4 illustrates the application of partnership in a particular sector. In terms of broader and more wide-ranging partnership agreements between the voluntary and community sector and government, the development of a compact or accord as a formal expression of partnership is a relatively new and interesting phenomenon. In terms of the model outlined in Figure 4.2, such compacts are aimed in particular at securing the foundation for partnership relationships between government and the voluntary and community sector. In England, Scotland, Wales and Northern Ireland, compacts between the government and the voluntary and community sector were developed in the late 1990s. A federal government–voluntary sector accord was introduced in Canada at the end of 2001 (Voluntary Sector Task Force, 2001). According to Phillips (2001):

> . . . the overarching goal of an accord is to develop a framework to enable relations to be carried out differently and better than before. It is a framework agreement between a government and the voluntary sector that articulates a shared vision, agreed-upon principles and mutual undertakings to shape and guide their relationship.

Good (2001) makes similar points and further elaborates with regard to the compacts in use in the UK:

> Their stated intent is to provide a framework to guide the relationship and mutual understanding between the two parties including recognition by the government of the importance of the sector to society. Such compacts are not backed by the force of legislation. Their force is moral, not legal. Their authority comes from the involvement and endorsement of members of both government and the voluntary sector through broad-based consultation and involvement.

Phillips (2001) also makes the point that compacts are both a framework document and a process: 'Experience clearly demonstrates that the process of getting to an agreement and the ongoing means for implementing good practices, monitoring and reporting are as important, if not more so, than the content of the document itself'.

5.2   The phases of compact development and implementation

Phillips (2001) notes that three distinct phases can be discerned in the development and implementation of a compact:

- *phase 1 – development:* drafting the text of the framework agreement, engagement of the voluntary and community sector and government on its content, redrafting and formal agreement

- *phase 2 – development of codes of good practice:* giving substance to the framework through drafting one or more detailed guides about what constitutes good conduct for both government and the voluntary and community sector, engaging all sides in a dialogue on the acceptability of the codes, and initial implementation of them

- *phase 3 – monitoring, reporting and compliance:* monitoring on both sides to ensure that the framework agreement and codes are being followed, public reporting of the state of the relationship and addressing issues of non-compliance.

In the development phase in the UK, the compacts were drawn up by joint government and voluntary and community sector working groups. The participation of the voluntary and community sector was co-ordinated by national umbrella groups (for example the Northern Ireland Council for Voluntary Action, and, in the case of England, the National Council of Voluntary Organisations). The compacts themselves represent an agreed statement of the general principles and shared values governing the relationship between the voluntary and community sector and government. For example in the case of Northern Ireland (Northern Ireland Office, 1998), the main elements of the compact cover:

- *roles:* defining the respective roles of government and the voluntary and community sector in the relationship

- *shared values:* outlining the common ground and understandings of the relationship. From the point of view of this study, one significant shared value is accountability, defined as 'being answerable to all relevant stakeholders in relation to the propriety of policies, actions and use of resources'

- *shared principles:* detailing the key principles underpinning the relationship, including interdependence, co-operation, anticipation, representation and good practice. From the point of view of this study, the representation principle recognises the right of the voluntary and community sector to comment on, challenge and seek to influence government policies. It also recognises that the advocacy role is a distinctive characteristic of the voluntary and community sector

- *commitments:* outlining the commitments made by both the government and voluntary and community sector to lend substance to the values and principles in the compact. From the point of view of this study, on resourcing the government commits itself 'to allocate resources to the voluntary and community sector in accordance with clear objectives linked to departmental priorities and to monitor and evaluate their use against criteria of quality, efficiency, effectiveness, equity, sustainability and accountability'. The voluntary and community sector commits itself 'to maintain high standards of governance and conduct, to meet reporting and accountability obligations, and to develop quality standards, especially where public funds are provided', and 'to develop systems which ensure accountability to both funders and users'.

As noted above, the agreed principles recognise the advocacy role of voluntary and community organisations. This is also the case in the Canadian accord where, under the heading of independence, it is recognised that:

> . . . the independence of voluntary sector organisations includes their right within the law to challenge public policies, programmes and legislation and to advocate for change; and [that] advocacy is inherent to debate and change in a democratic society and, subject to the above principles, it should not affect any funding relationship that might exist (Voluntary Sector Task Force, 2001).

After the compacts themselves have been agreed as high-level framework documents, the next phase is the development of codes of good practice. These codes outline recommended practice in more detail for particular activities. For example in England there are five codes covering funding, consultation, volunteering, black and minority ethnic groups and community action. The funding code is of particular relevance to this study. In the English funding code, ten key points for an effective funding framework are set out and elaborated on in the text of the document (Compact Working Group, 2000). The ten key points are:

- value for money
- procedures that are consistent with the principles of good regulation and the need to provide effective protection of, and proper accountability for, public money
- respect for the sector's independence
- improved sustainability and longer-term planning, for example through multi-year roll-forward funding
- recognition of core costs and the different ways these can be met
- support for the sector's infrastructure
- fair access to strategic, project and contract funding
- improved co-operation and consistency between departments
- clarity in funding conditions
- joint approach to monitoring and evaluation.

In addition, the code includes detailed appendices outlining the process to be followed by government departments in assessing grant applications and a guiding set of standard terms and conditions on the use of grants received by voluntary and community organisations.

The final phase of compact implementation concerns monitoring and compliance. In the UK, monitoring is built around an annual review report to a meeting involving members of the voluntary and community sector and the government. In England the report is also presented to parliament.

5.3   Local compacts

In England progress has also been made in the development of local compacts between the voluntary sector and local authorities. Local compacts are designed to strengthen the relationship between local government and the voluntary sector and promote better partnership working. Work on the development of local compacts is co-ordinated by the Compact Working Group, a consortium of English national voluntary organisations also involved in the national compact (Osborne and McLoughlin, 2002). A survey undertaken in 2001 indicated that 60 per cent of local authority areas are 'compact-active', with 18 per cent having published a compact and 42 per cent developing one. A further 16 per cent indicated that they intend to make a start within one year (*Report of the Second Annual Meeting*, 2001).

5.4   Strengths and limitations of compacts

Phillips (2001) identifies three ways in particular in which compacts have the potential to improve the situation of voluntary and community organisations. The first improvement that compacts can bring about is in the everyday practices that government uses to interact with voluntary and community organisations. This can happen through the introduction of better practices within government departments and greater consistency of practice across departments. However, it is also possible that departments will fail to react or respond to the compact in practice, therefore expectations have been raised but the practice remains as before.

The second improvement compacts may bring is in changing the way government thinks about the voluntary and community sector. Here, the compact acts to enhance the autonomy of the sector and in particular its advocacy role. As has been seen, the independence of the voluntary and community sector is formally written into compacts. However, in practice government may emphasise the service-delivery role of voluntary and community organisations at the expense of their policy-influencing role. This may limit the practical independence of voluntary and community organisations (Young, 2000). Also, government's view of the role of compacts may change as the political make-up of the government changes.

The third improvement that compacts may bring is in enhancing the coherence of the voluntary and community sector as a sector. Through the process of engaging local organisations and groups in the development of a compact, national leadership may be able to improve trust and co-operation among the diversity of voluntary and community-based organisations. However, such action requires a strong umbrella organisation(s), which may not exist or not have sufficient legitimacy across the sector.

In practice, while compacts have been in existence for a limited time and it is too early to develop lessons from them, there is some evidence of overall positive effects to date. The first annual review of England's compact includes findings from a survey of government departments where 75 per cent said that they had seen a positive improvement in their relationship with voluntary and community organisations. A smaller number, approximately one-third of voluntary and community organisations who responded to a similar survey, said that the relationship with government had improved.

The second annual review, in 2001, also reports improvement on the previous year, but notes that there was limited implementation of the funding code within individual departments, with only 18 per cent of respondents saying that they found the code useful (*Report of the Second Annual Meeting*, 2001). Set against this, examples are given of how the funding code is changing practice in some areas, with almost half of government-funded organisations now being paid in advance and strategic three-year, roll-forward funding starting to be introduced across government.

Scotland has also reviewed implementation of the Scottish compact, based on questionnaires sent to the Scottish Executive and its agencies and to the voluntary sector (Scottish Executive, 2001). Of government departmental responses, 72 per cent felt that the compact was a useful reference document, especially the sections on funding and consultation. However, some concerns were raised around a commitment given in the compact to give the voluntary sector three months notice of funding decisions. In the voluntary sector, survey results suggest a limited improvement in working relationships, although 73 per cent recorded no change in the funding review relationship. On deciding and administering funding, 53 per cent recorded no change. Knowledge of the compact was also found to be low among local/regional voluntary organisations, with over 50 per cent unaware of its existence.

5.5 Conclusions

Partnership relationships between the voluntary and community sector and government are a growing feature internationally. Promoting joint problem-solving and decision-making approaches through partnership fora is now seen as a preferred way of working in many circumstances. In terms of this study, a key issue is how voluntary and community sector autonomy is maintained in the funding relationship with government. One way which partnership arrangements aim to address this issue is through the development of explicit statements guaranteeing the independent and advocacy role of the voluntary and community sector. The various UK compacts and the Canadian accord contain such formal expressions.

Similarly, partnership agreements aim to set out the main principles and commitments regarding the funding relationship between government and the voluntary and community sector. These act as general guides for how the funding relationship should work in practice. As compacts are a new development, the extent to which such formal statements influence practice is still open to question. However, initial indications are showing a positive but limited improvement in practice.

In Ireland, while there are no formal national or local compacts, the basic mechanism and processes needed to put such agreements in place, if desired, are there. The 2000 White Paper on supporting voluntary activity contains many of the items often included in a compact or accord. The main difference is, as Phillips (2001) states, that:

> . . . the White Paper is associated with a single line department, and therefore is seen to have less legitimacy or application across the (voluntary and community) sector, and its status as a framework document is regarded with some scepticism by the sector because voluntary organisations were not equal partners in creating it.

At a local level, the strategic policy committees of local authorities and/or the county and city development boards provide suitable fora for the development of local partnership agreements if so desired.

6

The role of contracting in the
funding relationship[1]

6.1   Introduction

While partnership at its best is seen as an inclusive process, the role of contracting in the funding relationship between the voluntary and community sector and government is often viewed with some suspicion by voluntary and community organisations. The term 'contracting' can conjure up images of competitive tendering, bureaucratic monitoring mechanisms and the like.

Yet governments are increasingly choosing to implement policies and deliver services through contractual relationships with agencies. This outsourcing of government services has long been in practice for those public services with a clear commercial orientation or equivalent. Thus for services such as refuse collection and cleaning, the competitive tendering and awarding of contracts is well established in many jurisdictions. Since the early 1990s, this practice has increasingly spread to the provision of social services. As Chalmers and Davis (2001) note:

> . . . the new view of welfare services . . . signals an outsourcing of services to organisations with roots in the community and a commitment to providing assistance for the needy. For instance, the Salvation Army, rather than a government agency, becomes the characteristic face of state welfare.

But often this move to contracting of social services occurs without a full understanding of the nature of contracts and contracting, on the part of both voluntary and community organisations and government organisations. To address this issue, a discussion of the different types of contracts and contracting follows, together with an analysis of some of the implementation problems and issues associated with a move to the

---

[1]   Much of sections 6.2 and 6.3 of this report is derived from Boyle (1993).

contracting of the funding relationship between voluntary and community organisations and government. Finally in this chapter, the current 'state of the art' with regard to contracting is assessed.

6.2   Types of contracting

Many people see contracts as agreements which are enforced or recognised by law. It is also common for people to associate contracting with a move towards the competitive tendering of services. In fact there is a range of contracts, of which the legal, competitive-tendered type are only a subset. Essentially, contracting can be thought of as occurring along a continuum from extremely 'discrete' to extremely 'relational' (Macneil, 1974). Figure 6.1 compares the two types of contracting on a number of important dimensions.

The discrete extreme of contracting is typified by very clear criteria: the contract is measurable, short term and focused on the substance of the exchanges which take place. The relational extreme, on the other hand, is typified by a long-term contract where exchange is not susceptible to measurement and where the focus is on the structures and processes that determine the nature of the contractual relationship. As one moves towards the relational extreme, the emphasis shifts from detailed contract specification to statements of the process to be followed when adjusting the contract: rules determining the length of the relationship, rules determining the response to unexpected factors that arise in the course of the contract and rules concerning the termination of the relationship (Goldberg, 1976).

For voluntary and community organisations and the public sector, the implication of the above is that there is unlikely to be one 'right' contract or means of contracting. The decision as to which contracting method to use will be influenced by the answers to the following key questions:

- What are the characteristics of the external environment, and in particular the number of potential service suppliers?

- What organisational resources are available on both sides – funds, time, personnel and expertise – to manage the contracting process?

- Is it possible to specify clearly service outputs and desired outcomes in the contract?

De Hoog (1990) has suggested three contracting models for public service delivery to cover the range of possible approaches in response to these three questions: the competition model, the negotiation model, and the co-operation model.

Figure 6.1 Differences between discrete and relational contracts

	Extreme discrete contract	Extreme relational contract
Measurability and actual measurement of exchange	One side of the exchange is money; other side is easily monetised; both are measured	Difficult to monetise or otherwise measure either side of the exchange
Duration	Short agreement process Short time between agreement and performance	Long term No finite beginning No end to either relationship or performance
Commencement and termination	Clear, agreed start and finish dates	Gradual
Planning	Focus on substance of exchange very complete and specific	Focus on structures and processes of relation Limited specific planning of substance Extensive specific planning of structures and processes
Future co-operation required post-commencement	Almost none required	Success of relationship entirely dependent on further co-operation in both performance and planning
Obligations and sanctions	Specific rules and rights applicable	Non-specific; based on customs or general principles

Source: based on Macneil (1974), pp. 738–40

Competitive contracting

This model is of the discrete contracting type and is used where there is a choice among several bids and where the one which provides the specified service at the lowest cost can be selected. There are two variants of the competitive model (Rimmer, 1991):

- *franchising:* the government acts as the sole buyer on behalf of consumers and, through a legally binding contract, confers temporary monopoly rights onto a producer. This process involves 'competition for the field'. With franchising, income usually exceeds costs and the contractor pays the tendering authority for the right to deliver a service

- *contracting-out:* involves 'competition within the field'. Expected costs usually exceed income generated in delivering the service, so the tendering authority pays the contractor to deliver the service.

The competitive model is likely to be successful where (a) there are a range of organisations that can bid for the contract, (b) the government agency and suppliers have the staff, time and expertise to engage in the complex contracting process of specification, monitoring and evaluation and (c) the nature of the service to be delivered and performance required can be specified with some degree of precision.

Negotiated contracting

This model is a form of relational contacting. The suppliers are often previous contractors or agencies which have expressed an interest in the contract. The desired services are not specified in great detail. Potential suppliers submit their proposals, the government agency chooses the preferred plan, and then negotiations begin on specific aspects of the contract, principally the price and the type and extent of services to be provided. In this model, the government and the contractor operate on a more equal basis than in the competitive model.

The negotiation model (a) can be used in service areas where there are few suppliers, (b) uses fewer organisational resources in the tendering process, but may be more costly in terms of monitoring and evaluation than the competitive model because the contract does not clearly specify performance standards and (c) deals with uncertainty and complexity by negotiating many of the details of the contract with suppliers in a flexible manner, allowing room for manoeuvre should conditions change.

Co-operative contracting

This model is also a form of relational contracting. Here there is typically only one contractor, and the government and contractor are relatively equal partners. The contractor becomes a key actor in assessing needs and planning and determining the methods and levels of service delivery. The government may be less inclined to enforce the contract through punitive measures, but rather to assist contractors in improving their performance. In place of a detailed contract specification, there is a flexible document together with a set of common professional standards to guide behaviour and practice. Contracts are awarded only where organisations have an established reputation for high standards of performance and ethics.

The co-operation model is likely to be useful where (a) there are few, if any, alternative service suppliers and it is unrealistic for the government to supply the service itself, (b) there is limited expertise and/or experience in service specification and monitoring and (c) there is difficulty in developing verifiable performance standards.

In practice, the distinction between these three models of contracting is not clear cut. A contract may contain elements from the different models, with some aspects of the contract being specified in a great degree of detail and other aspects based more on professional norms.

6.3   Implementation challenges associated with contracting

As well as being aware of the different types of contract, it is important to note that contracting involves more than just agreeing the terms of the contract itself. The contracting process between voluntary and community organisations and government agencies includes such issues as needs assessment and planning, the selection of service provider(s), negotiating and specifying the contract, managing and monitoring the contract and review and evaluation. The implementation of contracts thus involves a wide range of activities impacting on both voluntary and community organisations and government. These implementation activities may be divided into (a) ex-ante, associated with drafting, negotiating and specifying the contract, and (b) ex-post, associated with monitoring and evaluating contract achievement.

6.3.1   The ex-ante requirements of contracting – contract specification

A review of a variety of different contracts used in a public sector setting indicates a range of items commonly specified in contracts. These are set out in Figure 6.2 and some of the issues associated with these items are discussed below.

Figure 6.2 Items commonly included in contract specifications

---

Items commonly included in contract specifications:
- status, aims and objectives of the organisation
- delineation of responsibilities of contracting parties
- nature and level of service to be provided
- price to be paid for services
- duration of contract
- policies for service delivery
- quality of service standards
- accountability/monitoring arrangements
- mechanisms for billing, authorisation and settlement
- mechanisms for dealing with change and with disputes.

Status, aims and objectives of the organisation: the task here is to set out briefly the purpose of the organisation contracted to provide the services required, and the main objectives of the organisation. A key challenge is ensuring that the voluntary/community organisation's objectives with regard to the services under contract are in accordance with those of the funding body. Voluntary and community organisations and government may assign different priorities to objectives such as community service and efficiency.

Delineation of responsibilities of contracting parties: it is important to ensure that each of the contracting parties is clear about their respective spheres of responsibility. For example, decisions may need to be made on how pay rises and price increases will be dealt with.

Nature and level of service to be provided: this section sets out the specific type and level of service to be provided to designated persons or groups. It requires the funding organisation to have a clear picture of the needs of clients in order to ensure the provision of a satisfactory service. This needs-identification process is a difficult and time-consuming exercise, yet essential in clarifying expectations and requirements.

Price to be paid for services: in franchising, the government may choose to award the contract to the highest bidder, the bidder who promises to deliver a predefined service at the lowest cost or to the bidder who promises to maximise quantity and/or quality. In contracting-out, the tendering authority may pay for the total cost of a service or provide a minimum subsidy reflecting the difference between anticipated revenue and costs (Rimmer, 1991). For non-competitive contracts, alternative arrangements may be made. For example (a) block contracts, where services are provided to a defined population for an agreed fee, (b) cost and volume contracts, for a defined volume of services at an agreed price or (c) cost per case contracts for individual cases at a given price (Hulme, 1990).

Duration of contract: it is necessary to draw a balance between long-term contracts which may lead to a lack of flexibility and short-term contracts which may disrupt continuity of service.

Policies for service delivery: this area may include such issues as admission policy – the criteria used to include or exclude clients from the service provided. This can be a particular issue if a voluntary or community organisation has a selective policy with regard to admissions but government requires equality of access for all clients, including those with greater levels of dependency or behavioural problems.

Quality of service standards: quality is often seen as a crucial issue in the contracting process. The specification of quality standards is a demanding task. A distinction can be drawn between: (a) quality issues focused around the structure or process of service delivery (items such as waiting times, communications and decor) and (b) quality issues concerning the outcomes of professional interventions. It is much easier for the purchaser to specify quality standards for (a) than for (b). In the case of professional quality, it is more likely that contracts will seek to ensure that quality assurance procedures are in place.

Accountability/monitoring arrangements: issues to be covered under this heading include the information that the parties will make available to each other, and the form this will take, for example quarterly financial returns, annual reports and so on; the ability of the purchaser to make announced or unannounced visits to check standards; and representation on the board of management if applicable.

Mechanisms for billing, authorisation and settlement: whilst relatively straightforward, it is important that the means of dealing with billing, authorisation and settlement issues are agreed between the parties, as otherwise they can become contentious items.

Mechanisms for dealing with change and with disputes: the terms of the contract may need to be altered to reflect changing circumstances, identified by either voluntary and community organisations or government. This will be a subject for negotiation, but this process may be assisted if the potential need to address such issues is recognised in the contract. It is also common practice for contracts to outline methods of dispute resolution; these can include initial discussions between the parties, conciliation and arbitration procedures and, as a last resort, contract termination.

Overall, whilst the majority of contracts will contain most of the elements outlined above, the degree of detail with which each one is specified will vary according to the type of contract. With competitive contracts, specifications have to get into a great degree of detail. Contractors will not deliver any more than is specified. Vagueness about the nature of the service to be provided or the tasks to be undertaken can lead to an unsatisfactory position. With negotiated or co-operative contracts, the specification may be less detailed, leaving more room for flexibility and placing a greater degree of reliance on trust in the relationship between the parties. The danger with this latter approach is that if there are differences of opinion in what is to be provided by the contractor, the contract may not be specific enough to help resolve such conflicts.

6.3.2 The ex-post requirements of contracting – contract monitoring and evaluation

Once a contract has been agreed, the performance of the contractor must be monitored for the duration of the contract. However there are substantial problems in monitoring compliance. Questions to be addressed include: is the voluntary/community organisation offering a sufficient degree of choice to clients, are quality standards up to scratch, what is the level and nature of complaints from clients, are identified needs being met? There is a danger in the contract commissioner becoming submerged in detail. Yet if it is clearly too expensive to monitor everything, and decisions are made to restrict monitoring, some non-compliance may get by.

Basically, a decision must be made on the most effective control strategy to adopt. Organisational studies suggest two underlying control strategies: performance-based and people-based (Eisenhardt, 1985):

- *performance-based control:* this strategy suggests that something is measured: either the behaviour of contractors or the outputs and outcomes of those behaviours (Ouichi, 1979). Behaviour control is most effective when the task undertaken is readily programmable. Thus, for example, in processing money transactions if the correct behaviour is observed the desired result will automatically be achieved. Behaviours can be explicitly defined and readily measured. The behaviour of the contractor is the purchased commodity. Output and outcome control is more effective where goals can be clearly stated

- *people-based control:* this strategy is designed to fit situations where it is not possible to define the rules of behaviour and there is difficulty in determining a measurable output – a common problem for many social services. Here, the literature indicates that the selection policies, training policies and socialisation practices of the contractor can develop a social strategy for control. Thus the aim is to ensure that contractors select workers who are able and committed and pursue policies which reward those who display attitudes and values which lead to organisational success.

Whichever form of control is adopted, mechanisms will need to be set in place for monitoring progress. These may take the form of written reports from the voluntary/community organisation to the government agency, meetings between the two groups, or some combination of the two. It is likely that some combination of formal and informal communication channels will be most effective in securing co-operation, particularly for non-competitive contracts. Unless there are means of developing two-way communications, gaps between the intentions of the different participants may develop.

Evaluation also has a role to play in assessing the achievement of benefits through contracting. If monitoring is concerned with day-to-day activities, evaluation focuses on how things are done. The very need for the service, and whether it is the best means of achieving particular objectives, may be under investigation. The scope of evaluation encompasses the impact and outcomes of services or activities. Formal, in-depth evaluations conducted by the funding agency or independent third parties are likely to be costly and time-consuming affairs, most applicable to large-scale contracts either in terms of impact or the level of funding involved. For smaller contracts, in-house evaluation by the service deliverers themselves may be sufficient, provided the results are made available to the funding agency. These in-house evaluations may be supplemented by spot checks of more in-depth, independent evaluations.

6.3.3 The implementation challenges of contracting: an illustrative example

To illustrate some of the issues that can arise in contracting between voluntary and community organisations and government agencies, an example is set out here based on a detailed review undertaken by Lewis (1994) of the move to contracting of one voluntary organisation in an English urban authority. In 1990 the voluntary organisation signed a contract with the local authority for the provision of day care for elderly people. Prior to this, it had provided some day care under grant aid. The organisation had a federal structure, with the director of the umbrella organisation assuming responsibility for the contract and for local groups delivering the day care in four centres.

The contract was of a relational nature: no invitation to bid was issued to other organisations. The organisation had established a good relationship with the local authority. Notwithstanding this, the contract took nine months to negotiate and by the end both sides were taking legal advice. The main dividing issue was client access, with the local authority wanting to ensure access to the more dependent elderly, and the voluntary organisation wanting to maintain its policy of taking elderly people capable of walking-in but experiencing social isolation.

The contract as finally agreed was a mixture of very detailed specifications in places and less formal content in others. Some inputs, such as cleaning schedules, were specified in detail. Other activities were left more open ended. During the first two years of its operation, some elements were gradually specified in more detail. The management of the contract by the local authority was initially relatively informal and undertaken by social care professionals. This model changed during the second year, as the local authority moved to a more formal contracting process. A contracts manager was appointed from the private sector, with no experience of social care. While in theory this meant a move to a more formal management relationship, in practice the new manager's lack of knowledge of the field meant that the second annual review of the contract was less testing for the voluntary organisation.

The effects of the move to contracting on the voluntary organisation were very significant. The director felt that her job had changed completely, with an ever-increasing amount of her time involved in managing the contract. This required new skills, and aspects of the work could not be delegated as the federal office was staffed by largely volunteer, untrained administrators and secretaries. At the local level, the day care managers also experienced significant change. All four had previously provided day care under grant aid and two of the four were volunteers, the others being paid staff. One of the two volunteers tendered her resignation; she disliked the new administrative and monitoring requirements and felt that this kind of work had displaced her chief concern: the motivation of volunteers and clients. The other volunteer also disliked the changes, but carried on. Both the paid managers were more inclined to see the contract as a challenge and as keeping them 'on their toes'. Overall, as Lewis (1994) notes:

> . . . the perceptions of those most intimately involved with the running of the contract within the (voluntary) organisation revealed both that the shift towards greater formalisation and towards a more bureaucratic organisation were real and that the changes resulting from the environment of which contracting is a part are having a strong impact on the structure and culture of the organisation . . . Future growth of the organisation is likely to be geared to service provision which has implications for the broader goals of the organisation, particularly regarding campaigning and the provision of information.

While it is clearly inappropriate to generalise from one individual case, this example does nevertheless illustrate in practical terms some of the issues outlined above. The application of contracting is not a simple exercise. This finding is backed up by a wide-ranging review of the contracting-out of welfare services in Australia undertaken by the House of Representatives' Standing Committee on Family and Community Affairs (Chalmers and Davis, 2001). This review concludes that contracting had secured real gains in the quality and range of services being provided by non-government organisations. But it also identifies significant limitations. These include problems in developing appropriate performance indicators and in quantifying outcomes, a lack of consistency in standards and in quality assurance mechanisms, accreditation problems, high costs and limited expertise in contracting.

6.4   Contracting in Ireland: the current state of the art

The most comprehensive review of the relationship between government and voluntary and community organisations in Ireland, including the issue of contracting, is that undertaken by Donoghue (2002), which covers the relationship between 'smaller' voluntary organisations, excluding hospitals, and the former Eastern Health Board. While the review is limited to this one sector, the issues arising have a general applicability across the voluntary and community sector. This section therefore draws heavily on the issues raised by Donoghue.

In 1999, in a survey carried out for the review, Donoghue (2002) and a research team interviewed 58 voluntary organisations and 18 representatives of the former Eastern Health Board. The aim was to explore the nature of the relationship between voluntary organisations and the health board. While the survey addressed much broader issues than contracting, many of the points raised are pertinent to the presence or absence of a contractual relationship between government and voluntary and community organisations. For example, with regard to the decision to fund the voluntary organisation, while just over half of the respondents from voluntary organisations knew who the key decision makers were, little was known about the way in which decisions were made and the criteria used by the health board in choosing voluntary organisations. Similarly, communications with the health board were ad hoc and intermittent: seven respondents referred to regular/monthly meetings, fourteen said they met only once a year, eleven less than that and eight respondents said they had had no meetings with the health board.

Formal reporting procedures were found to consist of the submission of audited accounts and annual reports, if available. Apart from audited accounts, there were few procedures in place with regard to monitoring of standards and accountability. This was seen as a significant shortcoming:

> Most respondents, furthermore, from both voluntary organisations (46) and the Board (12) thought there was a need for the Board to put in place procedures to measure its support. This was attributed by respondents from voluntary organisations to the need for transparency and accountability in relation to public money (17) and also the effectiveness of service provision (17) . . . Several respondents thought that it would help voluntary organisations to plan their own services as it could provide them with knowledge about whether they were going to receive funding, and if they were going to be effective, while others thought that such procedures would be useful for measuring unmet

needs. A focus on qualitative and quantitative measures was said by respondents to be necessary in order to address both financial accountability and service effectiveness (Donoghue, 2002).

Overall, the picture that emerges is one where, with some exceptions, there is little or no structured engagement on funding decisions or the outcomes of funding between the former health board and voluntary organisations. Relationships are largely down to the practice of individuals, with systematic policy and procedures being absent. This may be seen as a rather extreme case of relational contracting, where there is an absence of many of the practices and procedures that would normally be associated with even a fairly 'loose' relational contract between organisations. However, from knowledge of the literature and from key informants for this study, this situation is not untypical of many relationships between government and voluntary and community organisations.

Interestingly, when asked how the relationship could be improved, respondents highlighted the need to move to a more structured relationship and one that was more formally contractual in nature. Three main components of a successful relationship were identified by both health board and voluntary organisation respondents. First is clarity, involving the setting out of clear objectives and expectations, with each party knowing why the relationship is in place. Some respondents explicitly mentioned the usefulness of contracts here. Second is parity of esteem or mutual respect and a sense of equality. Third is communication. Trust was also mentioned by a significant number of respondents.

The issue of contracts was explicitly raised when discussing the need for service agreements. These were in the process of being developed at the time of the survey, in line with the health strategy as outlined in section 2.4.4. Some voluntary organisations dealing with learning disabilities had some early experience of service agreements given the impact of the *Enhancing the Partnership* document, also discussed in section 2.4.4, which introduced service agreements in this area.

In general terms, respondents from both voluntary organisations and the health board were very much in favour of having service agreements. Only two respondents did not favour the idea. The main benefits were seen as providing a structure for the future operation of the relationship, providing clarity and setting out the aims and objectives of the collaboration. Agreements were also seen as a way of reducing the dependence on personalities. Interestingly, thirteen respondents noted that they had a service-agreement-type arrangement with other statutory bodies, which tended to cover guidelines about the work to be done, the way in which the work was to be done, the conditions of service, funding and reporting procedures. Of those thirteen, ten thought that this formal agreement had enhanced the relationship and had had a positive impact, improving transparency and clarity.

While respondents were generally supportive of the concept of service agreements, there was limited knowledge about how these agreements do or might operate in practice. They were seen as being a 'good thing' in principle, with the details yet to be addressed.

Contracting between government and voluntary and community organisations is at an early stage of development in Ireland. The historical base for the relationship is informal, unsupported by policy and procedures and reliant to a large extent on the practice and work style of individuals. Service agreements are a new feature on the scene (service agreements are also being used by the Homeless Agency in their funding relationship with voluntary organisations working with the homeless, as illustrated in section 4.5). There is broad support from both government agencies and voluntary and community organisations for the move to a more contractual style of relationship as illustrated by service agreements.

7

Moving towards outcome-focused contracting

7.1 Introduction

In section 3.3 of this study, demands for increased accountability for the use of public funds by voluntary and community organisations are recognised. These accountability demands have led to a more prominent role for contracting and the use of contracts between voluntary and community organisations and government. The potential dangers of such an approach leading to greater formalisation and more bureaucratic procedures are noted.

Similarly, chapter 6 highlights the role of contracting as one of the main mechanisms through which partnership arrangements between government and the voluntary and community sector are implemented. While partnerships may promote longer-term relationships rather than one-off funding allocations, contracting is seen as a way of helping define the parameters of the partnership relationship. Under the partnership ethos, there is an emphasis on joint decision making in determining the nature of the contract. That is, the contract is seen as more relational than competitive in nature. However there can still be problems with contracting in a partnership setting. Issues such as conflicts between organisational goals and those of the partnership may arise. Contracts may also focus the activities of a voluntary or community organisation on the main items specified in the contract, possibly to the detriment of the wider social goals of the organisation.

Given both the growing interest in and the concerns about contractual relationships, efforts are being made to promote the benefits of contracting and at the same time to minimise the associated difficulties. One particular development of note in recent years is the move towards contracts which focus on the outcomes to be achieved as the result of the contract. This is seen as a means of giving government assurance of accountability for the wise use of public funds, while at the same time giving voluntary and community organisations the freedom they need to be innovative and responsive. It does away with some of the rigidities imposed by a fee-per-item-of-service contract (for example a set amount of money for an agreed number of hours service), where the details of how services are to be provided must be addressed in the contract. In comparison, outcome-focused contracting aims to put more attention on the desired results (for example people placed in employment or a reduction in the number of unplanned pregnancies among teenage mothers), leaving it to the discretion of organisations as to how precisely they arrive at these results. The funding contract is geared towards what happens as a result of the funding.

In the remainder of this chapter, the meaning of outcomes is explored, together with the identification of problems associated with outcome-focused contracting. Examples of outcome-oriented contracts are examined to identify the role they can play in the funding relationship between the voluntary and community sector and government.

7.2   Defining outcomes

Most voluntary and community organisations will monitor the amount of funding they receive, both from government and other sources. They will also know how many staff and volunteers they have. Further, organisations will be clear about how services are delivered and the number and type of people receiving services. Organisations, in other words, can often make a good attempt at determining their inputs, activities and outputs:

- *inputs:* the resources consumed for a particular activity, for example staff, staff and volunteer time, buildings and equipment

- *activities:* what is done with the inputs to deliver services or 'how we work'. Sheltering and feeding homeless families and providing job training are examples of programme activities

- *outputs:* the direct products of the organisation arising from their activities. They include items such as the number of beds or places provided and the number of people provided with counselling. Outputs show the volume of work undertaken.

Traditionally, however, not many voluntary and community organisations attempt to systematically determine what happens to participants as a result of receiving their services. For example how many people who receive job training subsequently gain employment and are still employed one year later? How many people ensured that their children were vaccinated as a result of a public awareness campaign? Outcomes, as defined by the United Way of America (1996), are:

. . . the benefits or changes for individuals or populations during or after participating in program activities. They are influenced by a program's outputs. Outcomes may be related to behavior, skills, knowledge, attitudes, values, condition or other attributes. They are what participants know, think, or can do; or how they behave; or what their condition is, that is different following the program.

An important and useful distinction can be drawn between intermediate and final or end outcomes. Intermediate outcomes are interim accomplishments that are intended to (but may or may not) lead to end results (Hatry, 1999). So, for example, residents signing up to participate in an environmental improvement scheme is an intermediate outcome of a programme of training for tenants whose end outcome is a safer and cleaner neighbourhood. Intermediate outcomes are more closely and directly linked to an organisation's activities and outputs than end outcomes are, which may be influenced by a wide range of other factors and more difficult to assess.

A schematic representation of the linkage between inputs, activities, outputs and outcomes is given in Figure 7.1. This figure is a representation of the programme logic model, aiming to show how services are arranged so as to achieve benefits for participants. This model is increasingly being used by voluntary and community sector organisations, as well as many other public service organisations, to enhance their understanding of their performance.

7.3 Potential problems with outcome-focused contracting

Conceptually, the attraction of a focus on outcomes achieved by voluntary and community organisations is clear. Contracting for results achieved makes sense. However, such a move is not straightforward or without its difficulties. Frumkin (2001), in a review of the literature on outcome-focused contracting, identifies five broad problems and concerns:

- the danger of selection by organisations of those needing least support to achieve the agreed outcomes, marginalising the more disadvantaged or difficult to deal with cases. This process is sometimes referred to as 'creaming'. For example, selecting people who are most likely to succeed anyway to participate in a job-training programme

- the possible 'gaming' of the system: appearing to take actions without actually improving performance. This can happen particularly where activities are not closely monitored

Figure 7.1 Summary of programme logic model

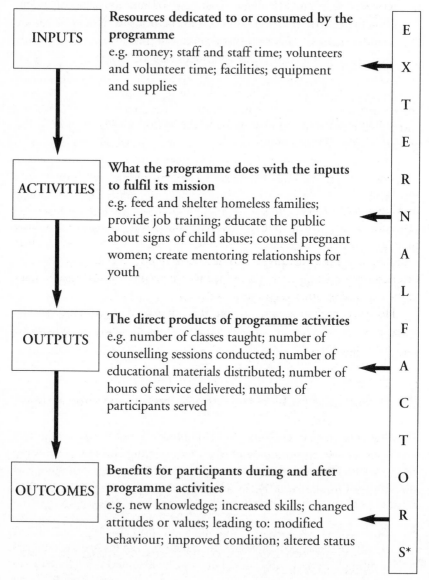

* External factors include, for example, economic and demographic change

Source: United Way of America, 1996

- many voluntary and community organisations have organisational cultures that do not see performance targets as appropriate for the services they provide. Mission-driven organisations may find it difficult or inappropriate to concentrate on specified outcomes that are seen as detached from their broad social obligations

- organisations may be concerned that they will become engrossed with the number of outcomes produced rather than with the quality of services provided

- outcome funding can place considerable strains on the capacity of the organisation to respond.

Such concerns are mirrored in a survey undertaken by the United Way of America (2000) of voluntary agency experience with outcome measurement. Of the approximately 300 agencies (75 per cent) that responded, just over half indicated that implementing outcome measurement had overloaded their record-keeping capacity. Just under half indicated that implementing outcome measurement caused resources to be diverted from existing activities and led to a focus on measurable outcomes at the expense of other important results.

However it is important to note that, despite these reservations, the agencies surveyed were in general supportive of outcome measurement. Approximately three-quarters of respondents either agreed or strongly agreed with the statements that 'on balance, implementing outcome measurement has had a positive impact on this program's ability to serve clients effectively' and 'program outcome information should be used in making decisions about program funding'. It is, therefore, important to recognise that problems with outcome-focused contracting need to be seen within an environment that is generally supportive of the use of outcomes in funding arrangements. Any system of funding will have strengths and limitations and the aim must be to minimise the disadvantages and to gain the maximum benefits from the perceived advantages.

7.4   Moving towards outcome-focused funding: some illustrative examples

A number of innovations in encouraging more interest in outcome-focused contracting have taken place in recent years, particularly in the US (Vinson, 1999). Three examples are reviewed below: milestone contracting in Oklahoma, performance contracting in Minnesota and social capital evaluation in Northern Ireland.

7.4.1   Milestone contracting in Oklahoma

This case study draws on an extensive review of the Oklahoma experience with milestone contracting conducted by Frumkin (2001). The case relates to the provision by nonprofit organisations of training services for people with disabilities on behalf of the Community Rehabilitation Services Unit of the Department of Rehabilitation Services. The aim of the training is to provide integrated employment for people with disabilities in the community. Interest in outcome contracting arose from the fact that placing people in jobs was seen to be both expensive and time consuming. The major cause of the problem was seen as the fee-for-service reimbursement structure, which put the emphasis on providing the services rather than on moving people into stable jobs. The implicit goal was seen as being to maximise the number of hours spent on a particular client.

To change the system, a milestone payment structure was devised and introduced in the early 1990s. This reimburses nonprofit organisations when clients reach a number of milestones along the way to getting a job. Reimbursement is for the average cost of providing the outcome rather than for the cost of staff time. The broad structure of the milestones and associated payments (with the largest payment for the final milestone) are listed in Figure 7.2.

Figure 7.2   Milestone contracting in Oklahoma

Milestone	Percentage of funding payment
Determination of need	10
Vocational preparation	10
Placement	10
Four-week job training	10
Ten-week job retention	15
Stabilisation	20
Full employment for 17 weeks and 90 days	25

Source: Frumkin (2001)

The first five milestones can be seen as intermediate outcomes, the sequence of steps needed to secure the final outcome of stable full-time employment. To avoid problems of 'creaming', a two-tier system of payments was introduced, where organisations receive higher fees for serving people designated as highly challenged.

In broad terms, the move has been very successful. A survey conducted in 1997 indicated that 13 of 16 nonprofit organisations surveyed showed improvements in the time taken to place people with disabilities in jobs and reductions in costs and paperwork. The initiative was seen as a good or excellent one by 75 per cent of the organisations surveyed. In 2000, the cost to government of closure of a case was $10,740 on average, compared to $22,000 in 1991. Most of the nonprofit organisations felt that the less-onerous reporting requirements under the milestone payment system had freed their job coaches to spend more time with clients. It had also enabled managers to spend more time supporting job coaches and ensuring things ran smoothly.

However, this is not to say that the move was painless. One-third of nonprofit organisations noted that the changeover was challenging. Many were found not to have the skills and experience to run outcome-focused organisations. Some felt that the focus on job placement was too narrow and inappropriate for what they did, and dropped out of the programme. Concerns about potential 'creaming' remain, despite the two-tier payment system.

Overall, however, the move is regarded as a beneficial one, both by government and by the majority of participating nonprofit organisations. Linking payments to milestones (intermediate and final outcomes) has led to improved services in terms of job placement for people with disabilities, increased efficiencies and reduced paperwork and administrative burden for nonprofit organisations.

7.4.2 *Performance contracting in Minnesota*

The Oklahoma milestone-contracting case is an example of where contracting specifically ties payments to outcomes. An alternative approach is to develop contracts that do not provide direct monetary incentives for performance, but instead encourage improved performance by detailing performance specification and outcome targets. A job-placement programme run by the Refugee Services Section of the Minnesota Department of Human Services, as outlined by Vinson (1999), provides an example of this latter approach.

In this case, performance contracting was introduced in 1990. Each contractor receives a grant based on the number of clients it proposes to serve and the cost of placement per client. Contractors must submit a two-year work plan containing performance indicators with targets for all activities leading to job placement. Contractors regularly report information on job placements, retention and other activities, and receive a quarterly status report in return. If performance is lower than 80 per cent of target, the providers must submit a corrective action plan. If performance does not improve in the next quarter, contractors are placed on probation. Ultimately, contracts may be terminated or not renewed.

Minnesota's programme was rated one of the six top performers in the country in 1997. From 1995 to 1999, the programme increased job placements from 591 per annum to 1,136 per annum. Providers also frequently exceed their targets for clients average hourly wages, jobs with health benefits and termination of cash assistance because of earnings.

7.4.3   Social capital evaluation in Northern Ireland

As noted previously, many voluntary and community organisations feel that the contracting process insufficiently captures the breadth and nature of the work that they are involved in. In particular, their advocacy role, in terms of speaking out for their clients' interests and of community transformation, is not seen to be captured when monitoring focuses on service delivery issues.

In an attempt to address this issue, Community Evaluation Northern Ireland (CENI) are trying to develop evaluation practices that will value these wider and less tangible outcomes of community and voluntary organisations. CENI are using the concept of social capital to provide the framework for this (Morrissey, McGinn and McDonnell, 2001). Putnam (1993) identifies social capital as 'features of social organisation, such as networks, norms and trust, that facilitate coordination and cooperation for mutual benefit'. Higher levels of social capital are seen as producing more socially healthy and economically competitive societies. CENI propose:

> . . . that the elements of social capital (principally trust, norms and networks) are used to organise indicators that are specific to the different contexts within which voluntary and community activity takes place. Community organisations have frequently complained that statutory funders under-value the process outcomes that are specific to the sector. Conversely, some funders worry that an exclusive focus on a 'non-measurable' process cannot represent value for money and carries

a high opportunity cost. We suggest that social capital captures many of the process outcomes of community-based activity without denying that outputs and results should be monitored as well. Particular funding arrangements will have their anticipated outcomes specified in advance. The concept of social capital can capture the process aspects of the activity (Morrissey, McGinn and McDonnell, 2001).

In terms of capturing social capital, CENI suggest a list of indicators (drawn from World Bank literature), which reflect four levels of social capital: individual, organisational, community and civic.

Individual capital: developing skills, capacity and confidence, both of individuals within organisations and of individual beneficiaries.
Indicators: involvement in volunteering; interpersonal trust among participants; knowledge of community affairs; number of active group memberships; depth of active participation in groups; trust in own community's groups/organisations.

Organisational capital: developing organisations to the point where they can fully participate within a modern system of governance, particularly partnership structures.
Indicators: number of active network memberships; depth of active participation in networks; sustainability of group/organisation's effects; inclusivity of group/organisation's membership; group/organisational capacity; formal participation in inter-sectoral linkage through partnerships; depth of participation in partnerships.

Community capital: social capital for 'bonding' – fostering networks of trust and collaboration within the communities in which the organisations are located.
Indicators: depth of collective action undertaken by communities; range of collective action undertaken by communities; integration within 'their' collective action of communities' marginalised groups e.g. stigmatised young people.

Civic capital: social capital for 'bridging' – developing networks of trust and collaboration beyond the limits of the religio-ethnic spaces of Northern Ireland's divided society, i.e. developing relationships based on common citizenship rather than ethnic identity.
Indicators: trust in 'other' community; trust in sub-regional partnerships across ethnic communities; trust in regional partnerships across ethnic communities (Morrissey, McGinn and McDonnell, 2001).

CENI recognise that not all these indicators will be of equal relevance or applicable to all voluntary and community organisations, but suggest that the framework can be tailored and adapted as appropriate. The approach is seen as a way of capturing the added value associated with funding voluntary and community organisations.

7.5   Conclusions

Attempting to measure outcomes is not a simple or straightforward task, but in recent times some useful guidance has been issued (see, for example, United Way of America, 1996; Martin and Kettner, 1996; and Hatry, 1999). In particular, the use of intermediate outcomes, or milestones as they are referred to in the Oklahoma case study, represents a way of specifying and detailing the results to be expected from the funding of services by voluntary and community organisations.

Outcome-focused contracting offers potential benefits both to government and to voluntary and community organisations. The government's need for accountability is ensured by focusing on what is actually happening as a result of the provision of public funds. The values of autonomy and innovation for voluntary and community organisations are promoted by moving away from detailed fee-per-item-of-service contracts towards more attention on outcomes. The measurement of social capital, as promoted by CENI, offers the opportunity of capturing some of the less quantifiable but nevertheless important aspects of the work of voluntary and community organisations.

However this is not to say that outcome-focused contracting is a panacea. There are potential problems, including the 'creaming' of services and increased marginalisation of those most in need and a focus on measurable outcomes at the expense of quality. Sometimes the outcomes themselves may be impossible to assess or may only be known several years after the funding has been given. What is needed, it is argued here, is an increasing focus on the use of outcome-oriented contracts, but not a total reliance on them as the solution to the funding relationship between government and voluntary and community organisations.

8

Conclusions and recommendations: moving towards a framework for a new funding relationship between voluntary and community organisations and government

8.1 Introduction

As noted in chapter 1, establishing an appropriate balance between the autonomy of voluntary and community organisations and the public accountability requirements of government funding poses challenges. A number of approaches are being used to address this autonomy/accountability dilemma. This chapter sets out the main findings with regard to the present funding relationship and outlines a framework for promoting a more structured funding relationship between voluntary and community organisations and the government into the future.

8.2 Conclusions

Chapter 2, by way of introduction to the study, outlines the role and organisation of the voluntary and community sector in Ireland and recognises the broad scope of the sector and its importance to the Irish economy. In 1999 the voluntary and community sector received €1.267 billion from Irish government and EU sources. Despite this large amount of funding, the relationship between government and the voluntary and community sector suffers from the absence of a clear policy framework. However there is evidence of improvement in this area. The 1994 health strategy and 1996 Department of Health paper *Enhancing the Partnership* (the latter developed in consultation with voluntary mental health agencies) seek to begin to address issues of independence and ongoing funding. Similarly, the 2000 White Paper on supporting voluntary activity sets out a new vision for the relationship between the voluntary and community sector and government and develops a range of principles and practical measures based on this vision.

Chapter 3 examines the changing environment governing the funding relationship between voluntary and community organisations and government. Management reforms, in particular a growth in performance contracting, have influenced the government view of the relationship: there is an increased emphasis generally on the need to specify and identify what will be delivered in return for public money. At the same time, in the context of social partnership developments in Ireland, the participation of voluntary and community organisations as part of a partnership network of organisations involved in the delivery of services is increasingly recognised by government. The voluntary and community organisations' views of the relationship have been influenced by the need to maintain a balance between their increasing role in government policy development and implementation and their independent advocacy voice for the individuals and groups they represent.

Also, voluntary and community organisations are under increasing public scrutiny in their use of funds. The nonprofit nature of voluntary and community activity is no longer an accepted guarantee of the prudent and effective use of public funds. However there are dangers in accountability procedures becoming overly control-focused and mechanistic, particularly given the great diversity that exists in the voluntary and community sector in terms of the size, mandate and means of operation of organisations.

Chapters 4 and 5 examine the issue of partnership and its implications for the funding relationship. In chapter 4, partnership is defined as involving the development of jointly agreed goals, with common interests and ownership, with all parties also having obligations under partnership agreements. At the same time, there are potential problems associated with a move to partnership arrangements, such as conflicts between individual organisational and partnership goals and the unequal strength of participants within the partnership. A framework model for understanding how partnerships can and should work, developed by the Institute of Public Health in Ireland, provides a useful model for highlighting key issues to be aware of when negotiating funding in a partnership setting.

Chapter 5 examines how partnership arrangements can contribute to addressing the issue of maintaining voluntary and community sector autonomy in the funding relationship with government. In particular, international experience in the development of compacts/accords between government and the voluntary and community sector can be seen to provide one way of giving formal expression to the independent and advocacy role of voluntary and community organisations. Such compacts/accords can also be a means of formally setting out the main principles and commitments regarding the funding relationship between government and the voluntary and community sector. These agreements may act as general guides as to how the funding relationship should work in practice. Compacts/accords may be developed at both national and local levels.

Chapters 6 and 7 investigate the role of contracting in the funding relationship. In chapter 6 the increasing move to implementing policies and delivering services through contractual relationships is examined. It is important to note that there are different types of contract, ranging from 'discrete' to 'relational' contracts. Competitive-based contracts are only one subset; with service agreements commonly used between voluntary and community organisations and government agencies tending more toward the relational end of contracting. Whichever style of contracting is followed, there are practical challenges associated with drawing up, negotiating, implementing and monitoring contracts. While contracting can provide real gains in terms of securing funding and clarity about the quality and range of services to be provided, there are limitations that must be addressed such as developing appropriate performance indicators, quantifying outcomes, quality assurance and the costs associated with securing expertise in contracting.

In Ireland there is limited experience in contracting between voluntary and community organisations and government. In fact, the way decisions are made about funding are often unclear; there is little ongoing communication between government agencies and voluntary and community organisations about the use of public money, and reporting and accountability is largely limited to the submission and scrutiny of audited accounts and annual reports. There is broad support both from the voluntary and community sector and government agencies for the use of service-agreement-type arrangements to bring more structure and formality to the relationship.

Chapter 7 examines international developments in the field of outcome-focused contracting. Here the focus is on specifying and meeting agreed outcomes to be achieved as a result of the contract. This approach helps give government assurance about how public funds are being used. At the same time, it gives voluntary and community organisations more freedom to innovate by doing away with the rigidities that can be imposed by a fee-per-item-of-service-type contract. The use of intermediate outcomes, sometimes referred to as milestones, presents a particularly interesting and potentially useful way of detailing the results to be expected from government funding of voluntary and community organisations. Focusing on outcomes can also include assessment of the contribution of voluntary and community organisations to the building of social capital.

8.3   Recommendations

The above discussion highlights the need for a more structured approach to the funding relationship between the voluntary and community sector and government in Ireland. Several potentially useful approaches to improving the relationship have been identified, including the use of compacts/accords and outcome-focused contracts. But individual initiatives on their own are likely to have limited impact. To be productive, they must fit into a coherent framework for promoting a more effective funding relationship. This begs the question as to what this framework should look like. Figure 8.1 sets out the broad parameters for a framework, which aims to address funding relationship issues at three levels. Level 1 focuses on the relationship between the voluntary and community sector and government at national level, level 2 on the relationship at sectoral/local level and level 3 on the relationship with government agencies.

Figure 8.1   A broad framework for determining the funding
relationship between the voluntary and community
sector and government

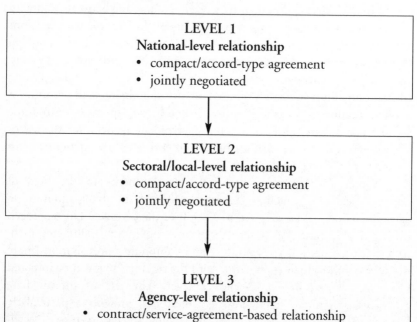

LEVEL 1
National-level relationship
• compact/accord-type agreement
• jointly negotiated

LEVEL 2
Sectoral/local-level relationship
• compact/accord-type agreement
• jointly negotiated

LEVEL 3
Agency-level relationship
• contract/service-agreement-based relationship
• monitoring and evaluation procedures agreed

8.3.1 *National-level relationship (level 1)*

> At the national level, it is recommended that some form of national agreement/compact/accord setting out the broad parameters governing the relationship between the voluntary and community sector and government, including funding, be devised.

The agreement should cover the general principles and shared values governing the relationship and recognise the advocacy role of voluntary and community organisations.

It is important that the national-level agreement be jointly negotiated and agreed by the voluntary and community sector and government. The 2000 White Paper on supporting voluntary activity contains much information that could easily translate across into an agreement if the relevant material were to be jointly developed further.

> It is also recommended that there is follow-up monitoring and annual reporting on the impact of the negotiated agreement to assess its usefulness in practice.

8.3.2 *Sectoral/local-level relationship (level 2)*

> As well as an overarching national-level agreement, it is recommended that at the sectoral (for example particular health sectors) or local (for example county and city development boards) level more detailed framework agreements be reached with the voluntary and community sector.

The *Enhancing the Partnership* (Department of Health, 1996) and Homeless Agency (2001) reports on funding arrangements provide examples of the type of agreement that can be negotiated here. Again, the emphasis in terms of process is on joint negotiation and agreement between the voluntary and community and government sectors involved.

> We agree with the recommendations outlined by Donoghue (2002) associated with the main recommendation for area health boards to develop a policy framework for their relationship with voluntary organisations, and suggest that her recommendations are applicable more generally to other sectoral/local-level agreements.

These recommendations state that:

- the policy must be designed in consultation with the voluntary sector
- the policy must contain procedures and protocols
- the policy must contribute to and thereby address relationship building
- the policy must also include procedures and protocols to address the maintenance of standards and accountability
- a central location in each area health board must be identified for the relationship between the area health boards and voluntary organisations.

More specifically with regard to funding, sectoral/local agreements should address items including: purpose and principles of funding, eligible services and activities, what is included in funding, application process and timetable, how applications are assessed, monitoring and evaluation procedures and an outline of the broad issues to be addressed in service agreements at the level of the individual organisation.

8.3.3   Agency-level relationship (level 3)

At the heart of the funding relationship is the working relationship between individual voluntary and community organisations and individual government agencies. While national and sectoral/local agreements help set the boundaries and provide some clarity on the parameters of the relationship, it is at the level of individual organisations that the ultimate success or failure of the funding relationship is determined.

> At this organisational level, it is recommended that the practice of developing service agreements be adopted as the standard approach and developed to provide a particular focus on the outcomes to be achieved by voluntary and community organisations with public funds.

Figure 8.2 sets out the main parameters for this organisation-level relationship.

In entering into negotiations on the production of a service agreement, it is important that each side does some prior thinking to ensure clarity of purpose as to why they are entering into the agreement. For the government funding organisation, this will require thinking to be done on the objectives to be achieved through the funding of voluntary and community organisations and the rationale for the funding in the first place. For the

Figure 8.2 Parameters for an outcome-focused funding relationship

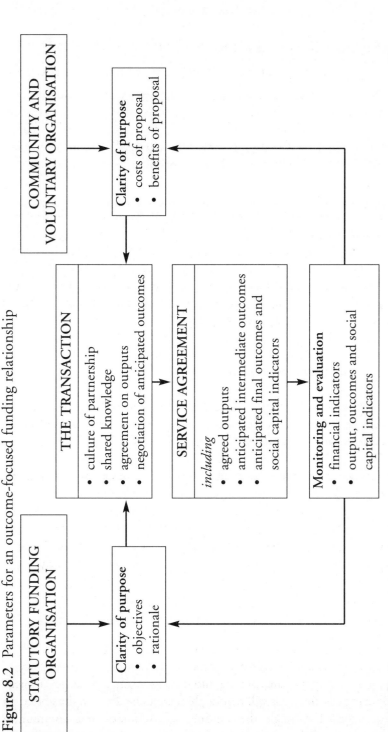

Source: adapted from Morrissey, McGinn and McDonnell (2001)

community and voluntary organisation, this will require thinking about the costs and benefits of receiving government funding and the consequent implications for the operation of the organisation.

The two parties can then enter into a negotiated transaction. It is important that this transaction is informed by a spirit of partnership, recognising the particular strengths that both parties bring to the relationship and acknowledging that there is a need to share knowledge held on both sides. The result of this transaction is the production of a service agreement.

> It is recommended that the precise nature of this service agreement is contingent on the level of funding involved.

When the level of funding is small (precise amounts can be determined at national or sectoral/local levels), the service agreement may need to be no more than a short, one or two page, document that indicates what is to be done with the funding and how outcomes are to be assessed. Where the funding amounts involved are larger, a more detailed service agreement may be required. Figure 6.2 sets out the main items commonly addressed in substantive service agreements.

> In particular, it is recommended that the service agreement should specify the agreed outputs, anticipated intermediate and final outcomes, and social capital indicators.

The agreed outputs required should be relatively straightforward. Developing agreed anticipated outcomes is likely to be more challenging. As noted by Morrissey, McGinn and McDonnell (2001):

> All outcomes cannot be specified in advance, since any intervention has unanticipated effects. Nevertheless, there is an obligation to indicate anticipated outcomes as the baseline against which the transaction can be evaluated. The indication of anticipated outcomes requires a synthesis of the different kinds of knowledge held by funder and funded organisations. Accordingly, they cannot be dictated by either side, but should be the result of negotiation.

The use of intermediate outcomes as outlined in chapter 7 represents a useful and structured way of specifying and detailing the results to be expected from the funding of services provided by voluntary and community organisations.

It is therefore recommended that particular attention be given to the development of intermediate outcomes resulting from the funding provided.

Similarly, the development of social capital indicators, where appropriate, provides information on what Morrissey, McGinn and McDonnell (2001) describe as the 'added value' associated with funding voluntary and community organisations, as specified in section 7.4.3.

Finally, it is important that there is monitoring and evaluation of the results achieved by government funding of voluntary and community organisations. As noted by Donoghue (2002), current monitoring and evaluation activity is ad hoc and often simply consists of voluntary and community organisations submitting their audited accounts and annual reports.

It is recommended that monitoring and evaluation procedures should cover financial indicators but also include output, outcome and social capital indicators.

Again, as with the development of service agreements, the level and scope of monitoring and evaluation should be linked to the level of funding and the capacity of the voluntary and community organisation. This monitoring and evaluation activity should in turn inform thinking regarding the development of subsequent service agreements.

8.4   Concluding remarks

This study was established to contribute to thinking on the development of the funding relationship between voluntary and community organisations and government. In particular, the study identifies the challenge involved in developing a balance between ensuring the continuing autonomy of voluntary and community organisations and the public accountability requirements associated with the use of public money. Recommendations are made as to ways of addressing this challenge, aiming to secure assurance as to the wise use of public funds while at the same time ensuring the continued autonomy of voluntary and community organisations.

Voluntary and community organisations play a pivotal role in securing the long-term welfare of Irish society. The voluntary and community sector has made, and continues to make, a significant contribution to the main social and economic issues facing Ireland. Many public services are delivered by voluntary and community organisations on behalf of government. Enhancing the relationship between the voluntary and community sector and government is important in this context. Securing a more effective funding relationship offers benefits for both parties. In moving forward, it is important that greater clarity and structure is brought to the funding relationship, and that this is achieved through the mutual exchange of information and respect for the different perspectives involved.

Appendix 1

Main organisations and individuals contacted and interviewed for the study

The Adelaide Hospital Society (Dr Fergus O'Ferrall)

Eastern Regional Health Authority (Pat McLoughlin)

Centre for Non-profit Management, Trinity College Dublin (Dr Freda Donoghue)

The Carmichael Centre (Kate O'Sullivan)

Focus Ireland (Mamar Zerouk and Eveline Fitzpatrick)

The Homeless Agency (Mary Higgins)

The Simon Community (Conor Hickey)

National Association for the Mentally Handicapped of Ireland (Deirdre Carroll)

CAFÉ

Disability Federation of Ireland (John Dolan)

The Wheel (Deirde Garvey)

Department of Social and Family Affairs

Department of Health and Children

Appendix 2

Government and EU funding of the voluntary and community sector, 1999

Government department/agency	Irish funding €m	EU funding €m	Total funding €m
Agriculture, Food and Rural Development	10.91	25.45	36.36
Arts, Culture, Gaeltacht and the Islands/Arts Council	0.29	0	0.29
Enterprise, Trade and Employment/FÁS	415.08	35.30	450.38
NOW	0	5.29	5.29
HORIZON	0	5.63	5.63
INTEGRA	0	4.31	4.31
YOUTHSTART	0	4.43	4.43
Defence/Irish Red Cross Society	2.99	0	2.99
Environment and Local Government/local authorities	55.99	0	55.99
Education and Science/VECs	25.40	0	25.40
Finance	6.40	0	6.40
Foreign Affairs	36.19	0	36.19
Health and Children/health boards	495.20	0	495.20
Justice, Equality and Law Reform	4.33	1.49	5.82
Probation and Welfare Service	6.41	0	6.41
Public Enterprise	0.15	0	0.15
Social, Community and Family Affairs	37.74	0	37.74
Combat Poverty Agency	1.24	0	1.24
Comhairle (NSSB)	2.88	0	2.88
Tourism, Sport and Recreation/ADM	31.38	32.57	63.95
Programme for Peace and Reconciliation (ADM, CPA)	5.08	15.24	20.32
Total	1,137.66	129.71	1,267.37

Source: White Paper on a Framework for Supporting Voluntary Activity and for Developing the Relationship between the State and the Community and Voluntary Sector, 2000

References

Boston, J., J. Martin, J. Pallot and P. Walsh (1996), *Public Management: The New Zealand Model*, Oxford: Oxford University Press

Boyle, R. (1993), 'Managing by contract in the public sector', *Administration*, vol. 40, no. 4, pp. 333–46

Boyle, R. (1995), *Towards a New Public Service*, Dublin: Institute of Public Administration

Boyle, R. (1998a), *Governance and Accountability in the Civil Service*, Committee for Public Management Research Discussion Paper 6, Dublin: Institute of Public Administration

Boyle, R. (1998b), *Partnership at the Organisation Level in the Public Service*, Dublin: Institute of Public Administration

Boyle, R. and P. Humphreys (2001), *A New Change Agenda for the Irish Public Service*, Committee for Public Management Research Discussion Paper 17, Dublin: Institute of Public Administration

Boyle, R., M. Butler and O. O'Donnell (2001), *Homeless Initiative: Final Evaluation Report*, Dublin: Homeless Agency

Brinkerhoff, J. M. and D. W. Brinkerhoff (2002), 'Government–nonprofit relations in comparative perspective: evolution, themes and new directions', *Public Administration and Development*, vol. 22, pp. 3–18

Butler, M. and R. Boyle (2000), *Service Planning in the Health Sector*, Committee for Public Management Research Discussion Paper 13, Dublin: Institute of Public Administration

Chalmers, J. and G. Davis (2001), 'Rediscovering implementation: public sector contracting and human services', *Australian Journal of Public Administration*, vol. 60, no. 2, pp. 74–85

Compact Working Group (2001), *Guidance for Public/Voluntary Sector Partnerships: A Proposed Supplement to the Funding Code*, London: National Council for Voluntary Organisations

De Hoog, R. H. (1990), 'Competition, negotiation or cooperation – three models for service contracting', *Administration and Society*, vol. 22, no. 3, pp. 317–40

Department of Health (1994), *Shaping a Healthier Future: A Strategy for Effective Healthcare in the 1990s*, Dublin: Government Publications

Department of Health (1996), *Enhancing the Partnership: Report of the Working Group on the Implementation of the Health Strategy in Relation to Persons with a Mental Handicap*, Dublin: Department of Health

Donoghue, F. (2002), *Reflecting the Relationships: An Exploration of the Relationships between the former Eastern Health Board and Voluntary Organisations in the Eastern Region*, Dublin: Eastern Regional Health Authority

Donoghue F., H. K. Anheier and L. M. Salamon (1999), *Uncovering the Nonprofit Sector in Ireland*, Dublin: National College of Ireland

Duffy, M. J. (1993), 'The voluntary sector and the personal social services', *Administration*, vol. 41, no. 3, pp. 323–44

Eisenhardt, K. M. (1985), 'Control: organisational and economic approaches', *Management Science*, vol. 31, no. 2, pp. 134–49

Faughan, P. (1990), *Partners in progress, the role of NGOs: voluntary organisations in the social services field*, Dublin: Social Science Research Centre, University College Dublin

Faughan, P. and P. Kelleher (1993), *The Voluntary Sector in the State: A study of organisations in one region*, Dublin: Community Action Network/The Conference of Major Religious Superiors

Frumkin, P. (2001), *Managing for Outcomes: Milestone Contracting in Oklahoma*, Arlington VA: PriceWaterhouseCoopers Endowment for the Business of Government

Gaster, L. and N. Deakin (1998), 'Local government and the voluntary sector: who needs whom – why and what for', *Local Governance*, vol. 24, no. 3, pp. 169–94

Goldberg, V. P. (1976), 'Regulation and administered contracts', *The Bell Journal of Economics*, vol. 7, no. 2, pp. 426–48

Good, D. A. (2001), 'A government voluntary sector accord', *ISUMA – Canadian Journal of Policy Research*, Summer, pp. 46–52

Hansmann, H. B. (1980), 'The role of non profit enterprise', *Harvard Law Review*, vol. 89, pp. 835–901

Harvey, B. and A. Williamson (1999), 'Series Preface', in S. Basini and F. Buckley, *The Meaning of Work in the Irish Voluntary Sector*, Coleraine: Association for Voluntary Action Research in Ireland, University of Ulster

Hatry, H. (1999), *Performance Measurement: Getting Results*, Washington DC: The Urban Institute Press

Hayes, T. (1999), *Government and the Voluntary Sector in the Republic of Ireland*, Coleraine: Association for Voluntary Action Research in Ireland, University of Ulster

Homeless Agency (2001), *A Clearer Future: New Funding Arrangements for Homeless Services in Dublin*, Dublin: Homeless Agency

Hulme, G. (1990), 'Contract funding and management in the National Health Service', *Public Money and Management*, Autumn, pp. 17–23

Huxham, C. (1995), 'Pursuing collaborative advantage', *Journal of the Operational Research Survey*, vol. 44, no. 6, pp. 599–611

Huxham, C. (1996), 'Advantage or inertia? Making collaboration work', in R. Paton, G. Clark, G. Jones, J. Lewis and P. Quintas (eds), *The New Management Reader*, London: Routledge, pp. 238–54

Institute of Public Health in Ireland (2000), *Partnership Framework: A Model for Partnerships for Health*, Dublin: Institute of Public Health in Ireland

Jackson, P. M. and L. Stainsby (2000), 'Managing public sector networked organizations', *Public Money and Management*, January–March, pp. 1–16

Kernaghan, K. (1993), 'Partnership and public administration: conceptual and practical considerations', *Canadian Public Administration*, vol. 36, no. 1, pp. 57–76

Law Society's Law Reform Committee (2002), *Charity Law: The Case for Reform*, Dublin: Law Society

Lewis, J. (1994), 'Voluntary organisations in "new partnership" with local authorities: the anatomy of a contract', *Social Policy and Administration*, vol. 28, no. 3, pp. 206–20

Macneil, I. R. (1974), 'The many futures of contracts', *Southern California Law Review*, vol. 47, no. 3, pp. 691–816

Martin, L. L. and P. M. Kettner (1996), *Measuring the Performance of Human Service Programs*, London: Sage Publications

Morrissey, M., P. McGinn and B. McDonnell (2001), *Summary of Interim Report on Research into Evaluating Community Based and Voluntary Activity in Northern Ireland*, commissioned by the Voluntary Activity Unit, Department for Social Development, Belfast: Community Evaluation Northern Ireland (CENI)

National Institute for Governance (2001), *Proceedings of Seminar on Accountability and the Voluntary Sector: National and International Perspectives*, 6 April, Canberra: National Institute for Governance

NESC (1996), *Strategy into the 21st Century*, Dublin: Government Publications

NESC (1999), *Opportunities, Challenges and Capacities for Choice*, Dublin: Government Publications

Northern Ireland Office (1998), *Building Real Partnership: Compact between Government and the Voluntary and Community Sector in Northern Ireland*, Belfast: Northern Ireland Office

Ó Cinnéide, S. (1999), 'Democracy and the constitution', *Administration*, vol. 46, no. 4, pp. 41–58

O'Donnell, R. (2001), *The Future of Social Partnership in Ireland*, a discussion paper prepared for the National Competitiveness Council, Dublin: National Competitiveness Council, Forfás

O'Ferrall, F. (2000), *Citizenship and Public Service: Voluntary and Statutory Relationships in Irish Healthcare*, Dublin: Adelaide Hospital Society

O'Sullivan, E. (1999), 'Voluntary agencies in Ireland – what future role?', *Administration*, vol. 47, no. 4, pp. 54–69

O'Sullivan, T. (1994), 'The voluntary–statutory relationship in the health services', *Administration*, vol. 42, no. 1, pp. 3–24

OECD (1999), *Performance Contracting*, PUMA/PAC(99)2, Paris: OECD

Osborne, S. P. and K. McLoughlin (2002), 'Trends and issues in the implementation of local voluntary sector compacts in England', *Public Money and Management*, vol. 22, no. 1, pp. 55–63

Ouichi, W. G. (1979), 'A conceptual framework for the design of organisational control mechanisms', *Management Science*, vol. 25, no. 9, pp. 838–48

Panel on Accountability and Governance in the Voluntary Sector (1999), *Building On Strength: Improving Governance and Accountability in Canada's Voluntary Sector*, Ottawa: Voluntary Sector Initiative

Partnership 2000 for Inclusion, Employment and Competitiveness (1996), Dublin: Government Publications

Phillips, S. D. (2001), 'A federal government – voluntary sector accord: implications for Canada's voluntary sector', paper prepared for Voluntary Sector Initiative Secretariat, Ottawa: Voluntary Sector Initiative

Pollitt, C. (1999), 'Accountability and democracy: answering to political authority and citizens needs', in International Institute of Administrative Sciences, *Accountability in Public Administration: Reconciling Democracy, Efficiency and Ethics,* proceedings of the first specialised international conference, Brussels: International Institute of Administrative Sciences

Preparing the Ground: Guidelines for the Progress from Strategy Groups to County/City Development Boards (1999), issued by the interdepartmental task force on the integration of local government and local development systems, April (www.cdb.ie)

Programme for Prosperity and Fairness (2000), Dublin: Government Publications

Putnam, R. D. (1993), 'The prosperous community – social capital and public life', *American Prospect,* vol. 13, p. 36

Report of the Second Annual Meeting to Review the Compact between Ministers and Representatives from the Voluntary and Community Sector (2001), London: National Council for Voluntary Organisations

Rimmer, S. J. (1991), 'Competitive tendering, contracting out and franchising: key concepts and issues', *Australian Journal of Public Administration,* vol. 50, no. 3, pp. 292–302

Salamon, L. M. (1987), 'Of market failure, voluntary failure and third-party government: toward a theory of government–nonprofit relations in the modern welfare state', *Journal of Voluntary Action Research,* vol. 16, nos 1–2, pp. 29–49

Salamon, L. M. (1995), *Partners in Public Service,* Baltimore: John Hopkins University Press

Scottish Executive (2001), *The Scottish Compact: Annual Review of Implementation of the Scottish Compact 2000–2001,* Edinburgh: Scottish Executive

United Way of America (1996), *Measuring Program Outcomes: A Practical Approach,* Alexandria VA: United Way of America

United Way of America (2000), *Agency Experiences with Outcome Measurement – Survey Findings,* Alexandria VA: United Way of America

Vinson, E. (1999), *Performance Contracting in Six State Human Services Agencies,* Washington DC: The Urban Institute (www.urban.org)

Voluntary Sector Task Force (2001), *An Accord between the Government of Canada and the Voluntary Sector,* Ottawa: Privy Council Office

Weisbrod, B. A. (1977), *The Voluntary Nonprofit Sector,* Lexington: D. C. Heath and Company

White Paper on a Framework for Supporting Voluntary Activity and for Developing the Relationship between the State and the Community and Voluntary Sector (2000), Dublin: Government Publications

Wilson, A. and K. Charlton (1997), *Making Partnership Work: A Practical Guide for the Public, Private, Voluntary and Community Sectors*, York: York Publishing Services for the Joseph Rowntree Foundation

Young, D. R. (2000), 'Alternative models of government–nonprofit sector relations: theoretical and international perspectives', *Nonprofit and Voluntary Sector Quarterly*, vol. 29, no. 1, pp. 149–72